POETRY AS THERAPY

POETRY AS THERAPY

Edited by
Morris R. Morrison, Ph.D.
Director
American Academy of Poetry Therapy
Austin, Texas

HUMAN SCIENCES PRESS, INC.
72 FIFTH AVENUE
NEW YORK, N.Y. 10011-8004

Copyright © 1987 by Human Sciences Press, Inc.
72 Fifth Avenue, New York, New York 10011

Printed in the United States of America
987654321

Library of Congress Cataloging-in-Publication Data

Poetry as therapy.

  Based on papers delivered at the symposium on the
use of poetry and the other creative arts in therapy
held at the Thompson Center on the University of Texas
campus in Austin, Tex., Nov. 1–2, 1984.

  Includes bibliographies and index.
  1. Poetry—Therapeutic use.   2. Psychotherapy.
I. Morrison, Morris R.
RC489.P6P628   1987   616.89′16   86-15281
ISBN 0-89885-312-5

This book is dedicated to Dr. Roger Williams—scientist, scholar, humanist—for his advocacy of an alliance between the creative arts and psychotherapy in sustaining mental health, and his perception of the inestimable potential inherent in this collaboration.

Particular recognition should be granted at this time to Margo Biesele and Leah Neal for their invaluable support.

5

Poetry in Therapy

Leave your calipers behind
Gentle reader
Your charts and radioactive salts
There is no textbook highway
To my heart
I orbit
Through the quiet
And unimagined spaces
Between my syllables
Among silent forms
And invisible shapes
You will discover me
Only
When you find your pulse
Responding to mine
In that instant
You will know
We were never strangers

Morris Morrison

To Poetry*

You shine on my bitter days
Like a sky full of stars
Like the sun that breaks his arrows
On a dark river,
My beloved poetry
Folds my soul into blue elements
So that I can be water,
Tempest, or flame.

*Reprinted, by permission, from Poetry therapy with disturbed adolescents (Morrison). In J.J. Leedy (Ed.), *Poetry therapy: The use of poetry in the treatment of emotional disorders.* Philadelphia: J.B. Lippincott & Co., 1969.

CONTENTS

7

CONTRIBUTORS

Adam Blatner, M.D., Medical Director, San Marcos Treatment Center, Brown Schools, San Marcos, Texas.

Gene Burd, Ph.D., Associate Professor of Journalism, University of Texas, Austin, Texas.

Paul Christensen, Ph.D., Professor of English, Texas A & M, University, Bryan, Texas.

Sheila Fling, Ph.D., Associate Professor of Psychology, Southwest Texas State University, San Marcos, Texas.

Betty Sue Flowers, Ph.D., Associate Professor of English, University of Texas, Austin, Texas.

Frances Cappon Geer, Ph.D., Professor of Psychology, Queensboro Community College, City University, New York.

Nene Sims Glenn, M.A., Historian, Houston, Texas.

Frances Louise Henry, Ed.D., Associate Professor of Art, Southwest Texas State University, San Marcos, Texas.

Grady Hillman, A.B., Director, Creative Writing Program, Huntsville State Prison, Huntsville, Texas.

Joseph Jones, Ph.D., Professor Emeritus, English, University of Texas, Austin, Texas.

Marc Kaminsky, M.A., Associated YM • YWHAs of Greater New York, New York.

Phyllis Luckenbach-Sawyers, M.A., Professor of Art, Southwest Texas State University, San Marcos, Texas.

Millicent Marcus, Ph.D., Associate Professor of Italian, Unversity of Texas, Austin, Texas.

Morris R. Morrison, Ph.D., Director, American Academy of Poetry Therapy, Austin, Texas; President Emeritus of the National Association for Poetry Therapy, New York.

Theresa G. Morrison, C.P.T., C.R.E., Certified Rehabilitation Counselor, Austin, Texas.

William Sutherland, Ph.D., Professor of English, University of Texas, Austin, Texas.

Charles Taylor, Ph.D., Instructor, Department of English, University of Texas, Austin, Texas.

Betty Vreeman, Ph.D., Assistant Professor of Drama, University of Texas, Austin, Texas.

John F. Whitaker, M.D., Department of Psychiatry, University of Texas, Health Science Center, Southwestern Medical School, Dallas, Texas.

Roger J. Williams, Ph.D., Professor Emeritus, Department of Biochemistry, University of Texas, Austin; Research Scientist, Clayton Foundation; Award Winner, Arthur M. Sackler Foundation for the Arts, Sciences, and the Humanities, as "pioneer" researcher, humanist, and teacher.

ACKNOWLEDGMENTS

We wish to thank the coauthors of this book, whose chapters are based on papers delivered at the symposium on the use of poetry and the other creative arts in therapy, held at the Thompson Center on the University of Texas campus in Austin, Texas, November 1 and 2, 1984, for their contributions to the conference. We also acknowledge our indebtedness to the following: Dr. Inez Jeffery who chaired the symposium; Larry Lyall and Leah Neal for their part in organizing the event; Sister Madeline Sophie Weber of the Departments of Psychology and Gerontology at St. Edward's University; Tracy Claflin, Department of Expressive Therapies, Austin Community College; and Marvella Woodruff, The Institute for Life Time Learning in Austin, for their active support in mailings and registration; to the Clayton Foundation, St. Edward's University, the National Association for Poetry Therapy, the Austin Writers League, and the Texas Circuit for their cosponsorship of the event.

We express our gratitude to Lucy Dubose and Lee Fuller of the Austin Movement Center for their film presentation; to Wanda Holland for her performance of Black poetry; to Marc Kaminsky for his poems *A Table of People,* and *The Road from*

Hiroshima, given a deeply moving reading by Arthur Strimling; to Dr. Ricardo Sanchez for his contribution to prison poetry, to Nadine Markova of Mexico City for sharing her films, *Hymn to Aton* and *Mother to Daughter,* award-winning documentaries now part of the permanent collection of the University of Texas Film Library.

FOREWORD

While all my scientific work has recognized and even underscored the reality and importance of material things, I believe that an increasing attention must be paid to the nonmaterial, unseen principles which influence the material things in the universe to behave as they do. Ideas, music, aspirations, poetry, conscience, and the love of beauty are all facts in the realm of human biology and are just as real as bones, flesh, proteins, enzymes, and hormones or the energy from the sun.

Therefore it was with pleasure that I, as a representative of the Clayton Foundation Biochemical Institute, agreed to help sponsor a symposium on the use of poetry and other creative arts in healing. This event, which led to the publication of this book, was cosponsored by a number of local universities and the American Academy of Poetry Therapy. It was held at the Joe C. Thompson Conference Center on the campus of The University of Texas at Austin in November, 1984.

Unshackled science and scholarship together need to recognize the undeniable fact that besides many material things in the human environment which we readily recognize there are numerous unseen, essential nonmaterial influences which abound and help make the universe what it is. These include love, hatred, hope, aspirations, fear, courage, a sense of decency and virtue, honesty and integrity, death, and even life itself—the very domain of the arts and the humanities.

Roger J. Williams, Ph.D.

PREFACE

To properly appreciate the place of the creative therapies, consider the entire range of psychotherapies in the broader context of the nature of personal growth and change. A holistic view focuses on far more then simply trying to solve a single problem. Emotional disturbances almost always involve a number of interdependent systems. It is not simply the nature of the stress which precipitates a disorder, so much as the presence of a number of factors which have interfered with the natural processes of healing. The level of social integration, the breadth of vocational and avocational roles, the person's spiritual vitality or lack thereof, the state of bodily health, and the range of interpersonal coping skills are all crucial factors which are all too often neglected in contemporary case formulations.

In other words, psychiatric disturbances are not simply a matter of weakness in a specific aspect of life, but rather reflect a lack of health in a variety of other systems which could otherwise compensate for the specific weakness. The challenge, therefore, is not merely "solving a problem" by means of "insight," but in most cases requires a program of empowerment which develops the patient's abilities in several areas.

In cultures with less elaborate technologies than ours, native healers often use a combination of approaches. For example, shamanistic healing may involve both a kind of exorcism and a form of empowerment through the shaman's helping his patients to reconnect with their spiritual heritage, the power of their totem animals, the value of finding a power song or some other symbolic mode of socio-spiritual support. The excorcism of intrusive spirits or other magical curses is in some ways analogous to the Western belief in the power of the psychical influence of parental attitudes, and the need for these influences to be "analyzed"—i.e., re-evaluated in the light of explicit consciousness. Yet such exorcism is not enough. Understanding the source of self-defeating cognitions must be complemented by the learning of new beliefs and behaviors, and such learning involves a variety of roles within the holistic system.

Another way to regard this general concept is to recognize the essential multidimensionality of human experience. A recent theory that expresses this idea centers on the different functions of the two hemispheres of the brain. In the last few centuries our culture has come to overemphasize the functioning of the left hemisphere, the part which deals primarily with verbal, logical, and linear modes of thought. We have come to appreciate the importance of the right hemisphere as well and this means that the major functions of aesthetic appreciation, musical and imaginative expression, and emotional experience are more highly valued. A comprehensive approach either to psychotherapy or to general education must deal with the full range of human potentialities, and these include the more symbolic dimensions of artistic abilities.

The creative therapies can serve as a bridge to empowerment in the same way that many of the components of native healing rituals in other cultures help the patient towards a holistic integration with health and the tribe as a social unit. By helping patients to reengage their natural channels of vitality which express the processes of imagination, intuition, and kinesthetic involvement, these therapies serve to restore the individual's sense of wholeness. For many people these dimensions of self-expression tend to become neglected in the course of education, yet, in being reintegrated, they serve to strengthen a patient in psychotherapy by marshalling a number of the potentials for transformation. The arts deserve to be more substantively integrated into the processes of education, recreation, and even programs of modern business management.

Some of the power of the various creative therapies may be understood through the theories of psychodrama, especially in regard to the value of developing each individual's capacity for spontaneity. The originator of psychodrama, J.L. Moreno, M.D. (1889–1974), was the only psychiatrist of his era who consistently emphasized the importance of spontaneity as a facet of healthy personal and social functioning—a philosophical concept, as well as a psychological theory. When a group of people meet to share their aspirations, a form "soul-making" ensues (to borrow a term from the analytical psychologist, James Hillman). This process applies also to groups meeting to share other artistic modes of expression—singing, music, art, poetry, movement and dance.

Another function of the creative arts in pscyhotherapy involves the facilitation of mental flexibility, a capacity which then may be applied to the generation of more creative strategies in life and a broader perspective for insight into the patient's life situation. Employing a number of unfamiliar metaphors such as can be found in poetry or art, dance or drama, the patient finds ways of expressing the nuances of personal feelings. The indirectness of these methods also enables the patient to allow the creative forces in his unconscious to contribute more adaptive syntheses of attitudes and behaviors.

The creative arts are a valuable component in the armamentarium of any psychotherapist. The process of personal growth and development involves many aspects of human experience where the expressive arts serve as channels for integrating intellect and imagination, sensation and emotion, mind and body.

Adam Blatner, M.D.

BIBLIOGRAPHY

Anderson, W. *Therapy and the arts,* New York: Harper/Colophon, 1977.

Blatner, A. *Acting-in: Practical application of psychodramatic methods.* New York: Springer Publishing Co., 1973.

Blatner, A. *The art of plays: An adult's guide to reclaiming spontaneity and imagination.* San Marcos, TX: Privately published by author, 1985.

Coutney, R. *Play, drama, and thought: The intellectual background to dramatic education.* London: Cassell, 1968.

Fleshman, R., & Fryrear, J. *The arts in therapy.* Chicago: Nelson-Hall, 1981.

McNiff, S. *The arts and psychotherapy.* Springfield, Ill: Charles C. Thomas, 1981.

INTRODUCTION

At the opening session of a conference on *The Use of the Creative Arts in Therapy,* sponsored by the American Psychiatric Association in 1979, Dr. Bertram Brown, then Assistant Surgeon-General of the United States and former director of the National Institute of Mental Health, predicted that the use of the arts in treatment would "trigger an important revolution" since "they deal with all three levels of the human brain." The focus of the conference was on the theme that the creative arts therapies evoke responses precisely at the level at which psychotherapists seek to engage their patients and do so "more directly and immediately than do the more traditional therapies."[1]

At a meeting of the American Psychiatric Association on May 13, 1981, Dr. Robert Gibson repeated the points he had made previously at the June 28, 1979 conference at which Dr. Brown delivered the keynote address.

Major advances, Dr. Gibson said, have been made to establish a scientific basis for the creative arts therapies. Professionals in these fields have worked towards their status by: developing a body of scientific knowledge, accrediting training programs, establishing systems for credentialing and registration of practitioners, setting standards for practice, and instituting mechanisms for self-discipline and maintenance of professional criteria.

Yet despite these achievements, creative arts therapists have been challenged on two counts. Their therapeutic activities have been dismissed by some as purely adjunctive. On the other hand, the use of the creative arts for therapeutic purposes has been called a denigration of the artistic process.

Those who apply the "adjunctive" label regard the art therapies as busywork—diversionary, and, at best, a means of reducing anxiety. This failure to appreciate the therapeutic potential of the creative arts therapies is common among mental health professionals who do not recognize the current achievement in this field.

"Mental health professionals who hope to offer a full range of treatment should have at least a basic understanding of the creative arts therapies."[2] At times these treatment efforts are provided on an individual basis. More often, they are part of an integrated individualized treatment plan. To achieve the full potential of these therapeutic modalities, it is perceived that all team members should have a general understanding of the indications and the contributions that creative arts therapies can make to patient care.

Professor Norman Cousins, now on the faculty of the U.C.L.A. School of Medicine, commenting on current scientific research which lends support to Brown and Gibson, notes that the human brain is indeed "an apothecary capable of writing prescriptions" and that many of the problems of patients are better comprehended through the realm bequeathed by art and literature than through facts disclosed by sciences.

Dr. Jules Masserman, president of the World Association for Social Psychiatry, refers to the "aesthetic psychiatrist" and asks "Are there any others?"[3]

In *The Uses of Poetry*, published in 1978, the British scholar, Dr. Denys Thompson, informs us that from the earliest times music and poetry have been regarded as healing agents.[4] This function of the arts is traced by Thompson through biblical literature, the Egyptian *Book of the Dead*, the poetry of classical Greece and India, through Gaelic poetry, and the tradition of American Indian societies, and in the customs of pre-Islamic Arabs where "words in themselves seem to have retained their ancient and magical power."[5]

Thompson retells a fifteenth century tale from Persia about a poet who went to a doctor, complaining of depression and an inside full of knots. The doctor asked whether he had composed a new poem lately not as yet recited or published. The poet replied in the affirmative. The doctor then had him recite it a first, second, and third time. He then told the poet, "Begone, you are cured. It was this poem that was tied up inside of you; now it has come forth into the open, you have found recovery."[6]

The Scottish poet Robert Burns centuries later discerned a comparable insight when he observed, "My passion raged like so many devils, till they got vent in rhyme, and then coming over my verses like a spell, soothed all into quiet."[7]

After touching upon the global use of poetry as therapy throughout the ages, Thompson traces its first use in institutional care to the Philadelphia Hospital founded by Dr. Benjamin Rush, the father of American psychiatry. We are informed that poetry therapy has continued in practice there for the past 2 centuries.

A study published by Doubleday & Co. in 1978, *Poetry for Peace of Mind* by Alison Wyrley Birch, finds in 1978 at least 200 hospitals for mentally ill people in the United States and Canada with poetry therapy groups meeting regularly "with amazing results."[8] Dr. Henry Brill, psychiatrist and director at Pilgrim State Hospital wrote, "We are witnessing a renaissance. Poetry therapy was well described in ancient Greek literature. It still appears to retain its value for purging the soul and cleansing the mind." Dr. Luke, also at Pilgrim State Hospital, wrote that the use of the poem in treatment works "something like a miracle."[9]

The foregoing would appear to herald a significant change of climate from the days when Dr. S. I. Hayakawa, then President of San Francisco State College, was moved to exclaim, "I don't know why it has taken the healing professions so long to discover the connection between poetry and the cure of souls . . . One reason, no doubt, is the fragmentation of knowledge, especially in our universities, resulting in the conviction that literature is literature, and psychology is psychology and never should the twain be permitted to meet."[10]

In *Fragment of a Great Confession*, Dr. Theodore Reik, a former associate of Sigmund Freud describes how the poet and psychologist do meet and that he himself in his practice of psychotherapy had attempted to produce a poetry of psychoanalysis.

"The metaphors of the poet" he writes, "are often more meaningful than technical scientific language with all its precision and clarity. The psychologist is perforce content if he succeeds in expressing the processes of the unconscious approximately, even by an awkward and uncertain phrase. He must be satisfied if he somehow succeeds in capturing a little of the life of the mind. While the poet has created and given embodiment to this life even as he thought to conceal it. Poets and psychologists alike try to grasp the last secret of the human soul. They agree finally. This last is unsayable."

Reik's mentor, Freud himself, also understood the affinity between psychology and poetry when he credited the poets with discovering the unconscious before he did, and referred to the poets as "those few to whom it's given . . . to salvage from the whirlpool of their emotions the deepest truths to which we others have to force our way, ceaselessly groping among torturing uncertainties."[11]

In the essay *Delusion and Dream,* where he analyzes the novel, *Gravida,* Freud proclaims that storytellers are "valuable allies for they usually know many things between heaven and earth that are not yet dreamed in our philosophy." Elaborating further, Freud adds that in psychological insight, "poets are, indeed, far ahead of us ordinary people, because they draw from sources that are not yet accessible to science."[12]

As late as 1969, music, drama, and painting were still relegated to the status of ancillary therapies, and poetry was labeled "a relative newcomer to the adjunctive program,"[13] even though commendation is extended to therapists proposing that "the poet's intuition be accorded its rightful place among our methodologies for understanding and treating the ailments of human nature."[14]

It was not until 1979 that the arts in therapy were elevated to an equivalent status with the other psychotherapies. Dr. Israel Zwerling, chairman of the department of psychiatry at Hahnemann Medical College and Hospital in Philadelphia, had begun to urge upgrading the characterization of the arts therapies from "adjunctive therapies," a misnomer in his judgment.[15]

According to the psychiatric dictionary of Hinsie and Campbell, psychotherapy is defined as any form of treatment for mental illness, behavioral maladaptations, and/or other problems assumed to be of an emotional nature; in which a trained person deliberately establishes a professional relationship with a patient for the purpose of removing, modifying, or retarding existing symptoms, of reversing disturbed patterns of behavior, and of promoting positive personality growth and development.[16]

Dr. Zwerling contends that the creative arts therapies meet the terms of this definition. Moreover, the creative arts therapist is a "real" therapist, not an "adjunctive subordinate," since his preparation is specifically designed for the treatment of the mentally ill and emotionally disturbed. The arts therapist has received credentialing for his training and fitness. Zwerling refers to the careful balancing of training for creative arts therapists in basic and applied areas, including personality theory, psychopathology, and psychodynamics—along with individual, group, and family therapy as well in the application of his particular art form to the psychotherapeutic process.

On November 29, 1977, the *Congressional Record* in its publication of the proceedings of the 95th Congress features a commendation by Senator Javits of the use of the arts in therapy as "a means for the creative resolution of problematic behavior." He concludes, "we must recognize and advance the role of the arts as therapy."

The chapters that follow are based, in the main, on presentations made at the conference on the use of poetry and the other creative arts in healing, held at the Thompson Center in Austin, Texas, November 10 and 11, 1984. These papers represent contributions from a broad range of interdisciplinary scholarship in the areas of English and Italian studies, journalism, art, drama, psychology, counseling, education, and psychiatry.

It is as if these contributors had assembled to the editorial call of the *Texas Humanist* (May–June 1984), that together physicians and humanists can help us understand the challenge of the postmodern world and "more than ever, the humanities and medicine must be united."

References

1. *Conference on creative arts therapies.* Pamphlet published by the American Psychiatric Association, Washington, DC, 1980.

2. *Ibid,* p. 4.

3. Thompson, D. *The uses of poetry.* New York: Cambridge University Press, 1978, p.209.

4. *Ibid,* p. 213.

5. *Ibid,* p. 213.

6. *Ibid,* p. 214.

7. *Ibid,* p. 214.

8. Birch, A. W. *Poetry for peace of mind.* New York: Doubleday and Company, 1978, p. 4.

9. *Ibid,* p. 4.

10. Hayakawa, S. I. Postscript, Metamessages and self-discovery. In J. J. Leedy (Ed.), *Poetry therapy.* Philadelphia, PA: Lippincott & Co., 1969, p. 269.

11. Reik, T. *Fragment of a great confession.* New York: Farrar, Straus & Co., 1939, p. 211.

12. Freud, S. The poet and daydreaming. *Collected papers,* (Vol.4), London: Hogarth Press, 1953, pp. 173–183.

13. Wolberg, L. The vacuum. In J. J. Leedy (Ed.), *Poetry therapy.* Philadelphia, PA: J.B. Lippincott & Co., 1969, p. 9.

14. *Ibid,* p. 10.

15. Zwerling, I. The creative arts therapies as psychotherapies. Address to the Conference on Creative Arts Therapies, June 28–30, 1979. *The use of creative arts in therapy.* Pamphlet published by the American Psychiatric Association, Washington, DC, 1980, p. 2.

16. *Ibid,* p. 3.

Chapter 1

THE ARTS AND HEALING

Frances Louise Henry
Phyllis Luckenbach-Sawyers

Art is the visible shape of human development. Not only is it an unfolding picture of man at his most primitive; it also reveals civilization at its most sophisticated. Art gives form to the many faces of the legend, pictorial, epic, musical, and architectural. It is the infinite images of spirit, an expression and a tracing of the self. Form is the shape of content. Art as therapy, as self-actualization, and art for healing can be traced back in time to the Paleolithic era, to the early cave paintings which are believed to have served psychological and mystical purposes, readying the hunter's mind for the hunt. These early paintings offered as magic to the gods are analogous to the work of modern-day clients who bring their art to the therapist with a faith that through this act will come a heightened and more aware sense of reality. The earliest form of imagistic healing can be traced in the lifeway of the shaman across many cultures to its Paleolithic origins. Visualization may well be the most ancient healing technique used by human beings. In the beginning the shaman was identified with untamed creatures which provided the society's food, clothing, and shelter. This concept was communicated to Arctic explorer Nud Rasmussen by an Iglulik Eskimo.

27

> The greatest peril of life lies in the fact that human food consists entirely of souls. All the creatures that we have to kill and eat, all those that we have to strike down to make food and clothes for ourselves have souls. Souls that do not perish with the body and which must therefore be pacified lest they should revenge themselves on us for taking away their bodies.[1]

Ecstasy, which often accompanies visualization and meditative states, is a time-honored method of transcending our ordinary consciousness and a way of helping us arrive at insights we could not attain otherwise. An element of ecstasy, however slight, is part and parcel of every genuine symbol and myth. For if we participate fully in the symbol or myth, we are for that moment taken out of and beyond ourselves. The shaman's role encompasses many facets—he is physician, psychiatrist, seer, and spiritual leader. His ability to function in all these spheres rests on his power of visualization and imagination. In shamanic ceremonies rhythmic chanting and drumming help to induce a trancelike state in all participants, to invoke imagistic visions and a state of ecstasy.[2]

Among the Navaho Indians there is a legend of ancient shamans who had power to create sand paintings by speaking to the sand. The Navaho shaman creates highly complicated and traditional sand paintings. These are symbolic of the gods of the Navaho universe and of the patient's relation to them. The sand painting ritual lasts for 8 days; at the end of the ritual the painting is destroyed, brushed away. A Navaho *hand trembler* is part of the ceremony and is called in to determine why the patient is ill. While in trance, the trembler visualizes the cause of the illness. The patient then calls in the *singer,* or the shaman who sings or chants and draws with colored sand the images that will affect a cure. Often an *herb healer* is called upon, and this healer envisions the proper mixture of herbs for the patient. Art forms are also employed in shamanic healing, such as bones, shells and wooden carved charms or spirit catchers, which are sometimes worn around the neck. Animal masks are sometimes worn, and these too are to help the medicine person visualize spirits which could help in diagnosing and healing an illness.

The shaman as performing artist and healer activates the imagination to give form to an unpredictable cosmos. Psychic confusion is given symbolic form and the healing journey finds a pathway. Now the ill one has been given a language to express the seemingly inexpressible. The shaman realizes that life is power and energy, and he seeks to harness this ubiquitous and invisible force. These insights are timeless and are part of a primary phenomenon that illuminates the human condition.

Among Babylonians and Assyrians there was also a belief that illness was caused by evil spirits. Treatment included an appeal to the dieties to exorcise a demon from the patient. In these ancient cultures special priests were called upon to diagnose and interpret signs and omens from the sun and the storm gods. They paid close attention to the position of the sun, the moon, and the planets, studying with care the markings on the livers of sacrificial animals. Dreams and visions, however, played the most vital part in their healing arts. The ill person was also encouraged to receive a vision or a healing dream as he or she slept in a special temple. The patient would sleep in white, because white was believed to entice dreams during the temple sleep or "incubation."[3] An ancient Babylonian visualizing exercise to invoke a healing dream runs as follows:

> Reveal thyself to me, and let me see a favorable dream.
> May the dream that I dream be favorable, may the dream
> that I dream be true. May Mamu, the goddess of dreams
> stand at my head.[4]

The sun gods, depicted as winged beings, were consulted by Assyrian priest-healers. Fire was another important element in their healing techniques. A small sculpture of the demon-witch or sorcerer to be exorcised was created of wax, and the gods of fire were called upon to consume it. Another invocation for visualizing is this:

> Nasku, Fire God, great offspring of Anu, I raise the
> torch to illuminate thee. Those who have made images of
> me, reproducing my features, who have taken away my
> breath, torn n my hairs, may the Fire God, the strong one

> break their charm. I raise the torch, their images I burn,
> and every evil that seizes hold of men tremble, melt away,
> disappear. May your smoke rise to heaven; may the Fire
> God, the great magician restrain your strength.[5]

Visualizations for healing which were similar to the Babylonian versions existed among the Egyptians, Greeks, East Indians, and ancient Oriental civilizations. That supernatural demons and spirits were the cause of disease was an unquestioned
belief in early Egyptian culture. They had also developed a highly
complex system of magic, which it was said could control the
weather, divine the future, and bring people back to life. A ma-
gician-priest in a healing ritual would perform incantations which
were both prayers and visualizations. Osiris, god of the under-
world and the dead, Isis, goddess of fertility and motherhood,
and the god of the day, Horus, were all invoked in the healing
ceremonies.

In the evolving of human imagination there is a continuous
return to the realization of the unity and harmony of all things.
This awareness is mythologized and evoked through the rite
(from the Sanscrit word *rita,* meaning art and order or ritual).
Ceremonial rites and passages are the road on which one moves
to a wider phase or a larger order, as explained by Dr. Jean
Houston, psychologist and leader in mind research. She further
points out that stringent requirements in the ritual drama are
inherent to participation—service, commitment, grace, and a
giving-over are central. The self-conscious ego is dispelled before
the ritual can affect an art of grace and awareness. Rising from
our primal beginnings, the ritual is an evolutionary mode and
is a journey toward our own transcendence.[6]

Joseph Campbell writes:

> Form is the medium, the vehicle through which life
> becomes manifest in its grand style, articulate and grandiose.
> The mere shattering oof form is for human, as well as for
> animal life, a disaster. Ritual and decorum being the struc-
> tural forms of all civilization.[7]

Campbell also affirms that the only way any people has ever
arrived at a supporting and appropriately mature myth or rite

is through the insight offered by its own artists and its creative prophets.

In ancient Greek drama the ritual emphasized catharsis, which was of high significance in the form taken by drama. The word *katharsis* can mean a therapy or healing. In Western theology *catharsis* means as much as salvation. In traditional theories of drama its meaning is purgation. For the Greeks it was Aristotle who formulated the theory of drama as purgation. If the drama provokes a feeling of pity or terror for the hero's tragic dilemma, then the spectator is purged by his vicarious experience. Much of what we know of therapy and healing began in Epidaurus in the fifth century. Anyone in need, in those times, of some kind of healing, or *wholing*—the Greeks made no distinction between the two—or whose sense of reality had become confused, was apt to go up to Epidaurus. Upon arriving there, he would be amazed by the magnificent paintings, sculptures, and great temples. His eyes and all his senses were energized; he moved into a period of heightened sensibility, of intense stimulation and excitement. He would probably go to one of the grand theaters; even today one of the most beautiful and best preserved is the theater at Epidaurus. There, along with other Greeks, he would watch the soul-shaking dramas of hubris, of guilt, of sorrow, and tragedy. The comedies too were played to appreciative audiences. It is sometimes said that those plays would now be multiple X-rated. There was the high comedy of Aristophanes—and through their laughter, as well as tears, viewers found their way to another level of understanding of themselves and of others.

Rollo May writes about still another dramatic locale called Delphi, situated on the side of Mount Parnassus in Greece. The Greeks erected their shrines in celestially beautiful settings. The temple at Delphi is especially magnificent. It is dedicated to Apollo, the god of art, healing, reason, and of psychological and spiritual insight. It is a place where one immediately feels, writes May, "the awe and the sense of grandeur which befits the nature of the shrine," because it was here that the Greeks could draw strength in surmounting their anxieties.[8] It was in this temple from the chaotic archaic age through classical times that the great god Apollo counseled through his priestesses. Here was carved in a great marble slab a portion of the Greek creed, *Know thyself*. This famous dictum has become a focus of psychotherapy

through the ages. Archaic Greek culture was in a formative period of change and unrest, and the shrine at Delphi offered citizens guidance and a sense of stability.

In the statues of Apollo carved at this time we can see the
archaic god with his strong, straight form, his serene beauty of
head, and his balanced features which reflect a controlled passion.
We also see a subtle, knowing smile—the "archaic smile"—on his
almost symmetrical mouth. This god was the symbol of order to
Greek artists and to other citizens of the period. The statue there
has an unusual feature: the eyes appear dilated, or wider than
normal in the head of a man or in classic Greek statues. The
poet Rainer Maria Rilke refers to Apollo's dominant eyes, with
their quality of seeing into infinity, in his *Archaic Torso of Apollo:*
". . . his legendary head in which the eyeballs ripened." Rilke
continues

> . . . But his torso still glows like a candlelabrum in which
> his gaze, only turned low, holds and gleams; else could not
> the curve of the breast blind you. Not in the slight turn of
> the loins could a smile be running to that middle which car-
> ried procreation; else would this stone be standing maimed
> and short under the shoulder's translucent plunge, nor
> flimmering like the fell of beasts of prey, nor breaking out
> of all its contours like a star. There is no place that does
> not see you. You must change your life![9]

Rollo May suggests that the prominent eyes express an intense awareness, ". . . a looking about lest something unknown
might happen," which reflects an anxiety that goes along with
the fomenting age.[10]

Music has also played a prominent role in the healing arts
throughout time. Among many ancient cultures music created
by humans was thought of as a prototype of cosmic sound. The-
ologians once believed that music was divinely created when God
first endowed man with speech, which separated him from all
the other animals. With the gift of song he was raised to a level
only one rung lower than the angels. It was once believed that
the human soul was modeled and attuned to the spiritual harmony of a perfectly ordered universe, so that man alone of all

creatures possesses the capacity to imitate celestial harmonies through musical sounds.

Greek life abounded in musical occasions. There were choral songs accompanied by dancing in honor of Apollo, magical cure dances like those still practiced by the Sufi dervishes of Persia (in which the patient was placed in the middle of the dance circle to receive positive vibrations and the cumulative well-wishes of those dancing round him). There were also sword dances for young warriors and wrestling dances for unclothed athletes. There were dances for Spartan virgins and choruses and solo songs presented during performances of the great tragedies.[11]

Homer wrote in the Odyssey that the Greek minstrel was the favored mortal of the gods whom ". . . the muse loved above all other men and gave . . . both good and evil. Of his sight she deprived him but gave him the gift of sweet song."

Plato wrote that music is granted to men for the sake of harmony, which having motions akin to the revolutions of the soul, can correct any discord that has arisen in the soul's course. Music is to be the human ally in bringing the soul into harmony and into agreement with herself. Rhythm, too, according to Plato, is given by the muses for the same reasons.

The ancients tell of a time when the first humans could only sing like the birds or the winds; but eventually they forgot the melodies and had to begin to speak of words. Legends of Mexico and Peru tell of ancient masters of sound who could split huge stones in half with sound alone and then resonate them into place at will. According to legends, the Uxmal and Machu Picchu temples were built with elements of sound. Ancient Mayans, Hindus, and Tibetan Buddhists recognized that each person has his resonating frequency, which when sounded and heard could restore an ill person's health and sense of well-being. In China, a new emperor would call together his musicians and astrologers, commanding them to measure the exact length of the Imperial pipes to insure that the music played during his reign would be in accord with the music of the cosmos.[12]

Among the ancient Hebrews all prophets foretold the future through meditative chanting. Miriam, the sister of Moses, was said to have had great powers of vision communicated in chanting. The Hebrews and early Christians believed the singing of psalms had healing power. In the Talmud a song is alluded to which protects the hearers from disease; and in the Old Testament King Saul's madness is allayed by the power of David's harp. All of these priests, prophets, and ancient shamans of sound had a similar philosophy: that music represented a microcosm of the harmony of the universe and through it the meaning of cosmic laws and the intelligence inherent were accessible. The etheric quality of music was a tincture of the essence which filled the cosmos. The rhythm of music mirrored the rhythmic movement of the stars and was manifested on earth in the cycle of seasons, in the days and nights, in the tides of the seas, and in the rhythms of the human body: hence the affinity among astrologers, healers, and musicians.

A legacy of non-Western music, the music of India in particular, demonstrates renewed interest in the ability of music to alter mind-states. In the last decade it has been established through testing that music indeed affects the mind-state and also can alter respiration, pulse, and other body rhythms. Stanley Krippner in *The Highest State of Consciousness* identifies 20 mind-states—six of which seem to be strongly influenced by music. These are: meditation, trance, daydreaming, rapture, and "expanded" and normal waking states. Music naturally affects the emotions and consciousness because it alters perception of time. Breathing, heartbeat and blood pressure are all changed by the element of time or rhythm in music.[13]

Poets have long realized the power of the senses to recall imagery and events long past. The senses can evoke connections between the smell of rain and the touch of a soft hand, the brush of a feather and the golden heat of the sun; and in these episodes of cross-sensing experience is enriched. If we listen intently and do not restrict or label too soon, we can experience this richness, *synesthesia* or cross-sensing, at will. Our minds will work as well-tuned synthesizers.

Freud wrote that the world of the poet or the world of the writer is one where fantasy is invested with a great deal of affect, while being sharply separated from reality. He notes that poetic art creates pleasure and can overcome feelings of separation and diminish barriers erected between human beings. "The writer softens the egotistical character of the daydream by changes and disguises, offering aesthetic pleasure. The true enjoyment of literature proceeds from the release of tensions in our minds."[14] He later added that through poetry the individual is able to separate himself from the group—as the poet invents the hero myth, who represents himself, and in this way he alternates between levels of reality and imagination.

Dr. Morris Morrison, Founder of the American Academy of Poetry Therapy, speaks of his use of poetry as therapy with disturbed adolescents. He writes, "The effectiveness of poetry as therapy is rooted in the power that all literature possesses . . . to assist the individual in his search for self-understanding and for emotional liberation."[14] He also notes that poetry is especially useful because of its unique qualities and its power to initiate an intellectual and emotional experience with exceptional immediacy—it is the poet's gift, the poet's special gift, to *involve* one with his very first lines. Morrison further points out that poetry, drama, and religion have all evolved from a common ritual whose purpose it was to annul the participant's awareness of separation and lift him to experience unity with his group and its spirituality. Poetry, he suggests, "releases us from the world of the particular into the healing ambience of the universal."[15]

The secrets of rhythm in poetry and in dance have been traced to a relatedness with our physiology. Rhythms in dance and poetry correspond to movements and pulsings latent in the human system, and evoke and bring them to consciousness. To one suffering a sense of alienation poetry awakens an awareness that another's steps have preceded him on the same road. This offers reassurance. Poets expressing their deepest loneliness, fears, and anxieties give voice to what we also feel within ourselves. This recognition can help lead us back from alienation.

> The wise man looks into space and does not regard the small as too little, nor the great as too big; for he knows that there is no limit to dimensions.
>
> Lao Tzu

There is a Sanskrit word, *mandala,* which literally means circle or center. A mandala consists of a series of concentric forms suggestive of passage among different dimensions. In its essence it pertains not only to the earth but to the macrocosm in the microcosm, the largest structural processes as well as the smallest. A mandala is the pathway between the two, symbolizing both earth and man—the essence of man composed of the atom and the galaxy of which the earth seems but an atom. Man may be projected into the universe and the universe into man through the concept of the mandala.[16] The mandala has been manifested in the art forms and rituals of humankind since our earliest beginnings. It has been an integrative and meditative symbol for many cultures. To Westerners the reintroduction of the mandala concept can be credited primarily to the work of Carl Gustav Jung. He rediscovered the mandala as a basic structural form in the alchemical tradition. It occurred naturally and often as an integrative, healing art form which his patients created in their search for individuation. In *The Secret of the Golden Flower*, Jung and Richard C. Wilhelm compare and relate the idea of the mandala as a therapeutic device to the employment of the mandala in ritual and meditation. In either case the aim is to achieve a higher level of centeredness and integration.[16]

In the Orient the mandala has been viewed chiefly as a vehicle for concentrating the mind as a ritual instrument, allowing it to transcend its usual restrictions. The mandala has been used in the Western world as a therapeutic tool. By projecting his mental complexities upon the cosmic mandala grid, a patient is enabled to liberate and integrate his mind. The fact that the mandala and other archetypal images have a definite therapeutic effect on the individual has been empirically proved.[17] Often these images and structural forms represent attempts to see and put together apparently incompatible opposites, to bridge impossible chasms. The mere effort in this direction usually has a healing effect if it is done spontaneously.

Art therapy began as a movement in America in the mid-twentieth century as educators and psychologists began to view the art product as an indicator of the psychological and mental states of an individual. In 1926 Florence Goodenaugh published *The Measure of Intelligence in Drawing*, which has become a classic among educators and theorists. Other pioneers in the field were Rose Alschuler and LaBerta Hatwick, whose two-volume work was based on meaning in the graphic work of preschoolers, and

Viktor Lowenfeld, who published *Creative and Mental Growth* in 1947, a work based on the developmental stages of children as seen in their art work. Margaret Naumberg became in 1965 an important leader who devoted an analytical approach to art therapy in her work based on the psychology of Freud, stressing the release of the unconscious mind through the use of self-expression in art. Edith Kramer was also a major pioneer in art therapy. She believed healing resulted from the act of creating a work of art.[18]

At present there are various approaches to art as therapy. The technique called "Family Art Therapy" was developed by Hanna Kwiatkowska in 1967. Other therapists use a diagnostic-prescriptive method, and there are approaches of crisis intervention, socialization, and recreation. In addition to a National Art Therapy Association, national associations of dance therapy, music therapy, and poetry therapy all flourish, and there is great interest in the movement of psychodrama.

Another twentieth century theorist who influenced present-day art therapies is Alfred Adler. In Adlerian psychotherapy the discouraged individual is encouraged to discover new life interests, to self-actualize and choose his posture toward life. This wholistic view of *creative becoming* corresponds closely to that of contemporary art therapists, such as Janie Rhyne. Rhyne has written in *The Gestalt Art Experience:*

> Healthy children are natural gestaltists; they live in the present, give full attention to what they are doing, do what they want to do, trust their own experiential data, and until they are trained out of it; they know what they know with direct simplicity and accuracy.[19]

Mary Caroline Richards, poet, potter, and teacher, tells of a child who asked to play with clay figures in a Christmas manger scene. She says that the figures were colorful and beautiful and that with them was a tiny clay angel. She writes that the child moved the figures around on a low table, talking to herself and making up stories. . . . "Here are the people in a circle around the baby, and now they're walking aside in small groups; now two are coming back to take care of the baby who is crying, and now they're whispering quietly." She calls them, Husband, King, Woman, Baby, Angel, Sheep. One of the sheep, she says, wants a jewel from the King's box of gold. Mary Caroline writes:

> As I listened and entered in I felt a larger presence. It was like a poem fully sung. This child, Ruth, the improvised place, space, the beings who formed their stories in her thoughts, the primal quality of truth we human beings share, and the way it finds us. . . . Oh, how active the life spirit is in each small person, in each of us, and in all of the millions who live life on this earth, doing its work, suffering its conflicts, manifesting its human destiny and imagining. The whole world is our religion. We are blessed with an inner child; we may see it new.[20]

REFERENCES

1. Halifax, J. Shaman's journey. *Dromenon: Journal of New Ways of Being,* Spring 1981, *III* (2), 5.

2. Samuels, M. & Samuels, N. *Seeing with the mind's eye.* New York: Random House, 1975, pp. 209–210.

3. *Ibid,* p. 211.

4. *Ibid,* p. 212.

5. Jayne, W. *The healing gods of ancient civilizations.* New Haven, Connecticut: Yale University Press, 1925, p. 102.

6. Sawyers, P. L., & Henry, F. L., *Song of the coyote: Freeing the imagination through the arts.* Boston: American Press, 1980, p. 106.

7. Campbell, J. *Myths to live by.* New York: Bantam Books, 1973, p. 50.

8. May, R. *Courage to create.* New York: W. W. Norton, 1975, p. 95.

9. Rilke, R. M. Archaic torso of Apollo. In M. D. Herter, (Trans.), *Translations from the poetry of Rainer Maria Rilke,* New York: Norton, 1938, p. 181.

10. May, R. op. cit., p. 101.

11. McClelland, R. Music and altered states of consciousness. *Dromenon: Journal of New Ways of Being,* Winter 1979, *II* (3–4), 5.

12. *Ibid,* p. 3.

13. *Ibid,* p. 6.

14. Freud, S. *The interpretation of dreams,* New York: Basic Books, 1955.

15. Morrison, M. Poetry therapy with disturbed adolescents. In *Art therapy.* Philadelphia: J. B. Lippincott, 1969, p. 89.

16. Arguelles, J., & Arguelles, M. *Mandala.* Berkeley & London: Shambhala: 1972, p. 12.

17. Jung, C. G. *Mandala symbolism,* Princeton, N.J.: Princeton University Press, 1969, p. 5.

18. Kramer, E. Art therapy and art education: Overlapping functions. *Art Education,* April 1980, *33* (4), 16–18.

19. Rhyne, J. *The Gestalt art experience.* Monterey, Calif.: Brooks Cole Publishing Co., 1973, pp. 3, 4.

20. Richards, M. C. *The crossing point.* Middletown, Connecticut: Wesleyan University Press, 1973, p. 245.

Chapter 2

POETRY AND THERAPY*

Morris R. Morrison

In 1970, the Downstate Medical Center in Brooklyn, New York, initiated a visiting scholars program inviting notables outside the field of medicine to participate with the medical faculty and students in discussions related to the arts. Discussants at different dates included the historian Arnold S. Toynbee and the poets Archibald MacLeish and W. H. Auden. During conversation following one of these sessions, Auden was asked, "Is there such a thing as therapeutic poetry?" "No," he replied, "I don't think so at all." He followed this pronouncement with another, defining the goal of the writer. "The aim of writing," the poet stated, "is to enable people a little better to enjoy life or a little better to endure it."[1] Professor J. C. Coleman, quoted approvingly by Dr. Robert M. Goldenson in *The Encyclopedia of Human Behavior,* lists among the aims of psychotherapy "the resolution of handicapping or disabling conflicts and the opening of a

---

*Previously published as Poetry therapy with disturbed adolescents in J. J. Leedy (Ed.), *Poetry therapy: The use of poetry in the treatment of emotional disorders.* Philadelphia: J. B. Lippincott & Co., 1969.

pathway to a more meaningful and fulfilling existence."[2] In his act of denial Auden had unwittingly reaffirmed how germane are the concerns of poet and therapist.

Indeed, Auden's interest in Freud and psychoanalysis dates back to the twenties. Stephen Spender, referring to those days, tells us that at the time of his first acquaintance with Auden in 1928, he found him deeply concerned with psychotherapy and medicine. "At this early age," we are told, "Auden had already an extensive knowledge of the theories of modern psychology, which he used as a means of understanding his friends."[3] His friends and fellow authors, C. Day-Lewis and Christopher Isherwood, confirm Auden's parallel interests in poetry and psychotherapy. C. Day-Lewis writes, "Auden, while regarding so many of our actions as self-deception, yet believes, as I have already said, that neurosis is the cause of an individual's development. Such a psychological dialectic reflects itself in the paradoxes and the tensions of his poems."[4]

Christopher Isherwood tells of the great influence exerted over Auden by the American psychologist, Homer Lane, whose teachings are reflected in Auden's *The Orators* and *The Journal of an Airman.* Auden and Isherwood collaborated on a play, *The Enemies of a Bishop,* in which the hero, who represents sanity, appears as an idealized portrait of Lane. Auden had elsewhere enshrined Homer Lane, along with D. H. Lawrence and Andre Gide, as his spiritual mentor. Isherwood reveals the extent and degree of Lane's impact on Auden. "Auden was particularly interested in Lane's theories regarding the psychological causes of disease. References to these theories can be found in many of the early poems."[5]

In 1963 the Oxford University Press published a study by Professor Monroe K. Spears on the life and work of Auden. Allen Tate, paying tribute to the scholarship and intellectual powers of the critic, praised it as "the best book by anybody about a living poet."[6] Auden served as a behind-the-scenes collaborator. The dustjacket of the book tells us, "With Auden's cooperation the record is here set straight." Spears wrote, "I have taken some pains (and put Mr. Auden to some trouble) to make sure that I have the facts straight."[7] It must then have been with Auden's own endorsement that the statement was set down that "The notion of the poet as clinically detached, diagnosing the sickness of society and its component individuals, and of poetry as a kind of therapy performing a function somehow analogous to the psychoanalytic, is a fundamental in Auden's writing."[8]

Donald Davie in *Remembering the Movement,* a critical study of the poets of the fifties, many of whom were strongly influenced by Auden, wrote, "We conceived of it (poetry) as an act of public and private therapy, the poet resolving his conflicts by expressing them and offering them to the reader so that he could vicariously do the same thing."[9]

A poet for whom Auden has publicly expressed great admiration is Robert Graves. Reviewing Grave's *Collected Poems* in 1961, Auden confided that he had first read Graves in the volume of Georgian poetry when he was a schoolboy and that "Graves remained one of the very few poets whose volumes he always bought the moment they appeared."[10] Robert Graves says of his goal as a writer: "My poetry is, or should be, useful to me for one reason: It is the record of my individual struggle from darkness towards some measure of light . . . My poetry is, or should be, useful to others for its individual recording of that same struggle with which they are necessarily acquainted . . . Poetry recording the stripping of the individual darkness, must inevitably cast light upon what has been hidden for too long, and by so doing, make clear the naked exposure." He continues, "Freud cast light on a little of the darkness he had exposed. Benefiting by the sight of the light and the knowledge of the hidden nakedness, poetry must drag further into the clear nakedness of light more even of the hidden causes than Freud could realize."[11]

In *White Goddess,* which deals with the poetic process, Graves reports: "The pathology of poetic composition is no secret. A poet finds himself caught in some baffling emotional problem which is of such urgency that it sends him into a sort of trance. And in this trance his mind works with astonishing boldness and precision on several imaginative levels at once. The poem is either a practical answer to his problem or else it is a clear statement of it; and a problem clearly stated is half way to solution. Some poets are more plagued than others with emotional problems, and more conscientious in working out poems which arise from them—that is more attentive in their service to the Muse."[12]

Elsewhere, Graves wrote that poetry is formed by the supralogical reconciliation of conflicting emotional ideas during a trancelike suspension of normal habits of thought. The poet, he advises us, learns to induce the trance in self-protection whenever he feels unable to resolve an emotional conflict by simple logic.[13]

After he experienced an emotional breakdown during military service in World War I, Graves was treated by Dr. W. H. R. Rivers, a physician of exceptional, if controversial, talent. Dr. Rivers theorized that "every neurotic system like dreams, was at once the product of a mental conflict and an attempt to resolve it." Poems, he believed, functioned similarly. Reviewing his own poetry, Graves wrote, "My hope was to help the recovery of public health of mind as well as my own by the writing of therapeutic poems."[14]

Professor George Stade of Columbia University describes Graves's way of serving his Muse while looking after his neurosis: ". . . when he came to write in 1922 his first book of criticism, *On English Poetry*, based on 'evidence mainly subjective' . . . Graves advertised poetry as a 'form of psychotherapy' for the neurosis of poets and the culture they express and address. He assured his readers that 'a well-chosen anthology is a complete dispensary for the more common mental disorders and may be used as much for prevention as for cure.' A poem's rhythm puts the reader in a hypnotic trance; he is confronted with an allegorical solution of the problem that has been troubling him; his unconscious accepts the allegory as applicable to his own condition; the emotional crisis is relieved."[15] Professor Stade discusses the 20 years during which Graves "brought his poetic self into being through poems of self-definition and extrication."[16] This brings to mind Coleman's stated purpose of therapy: a better delineation of one's own identity and the opening of a pathway to a more meaningful and fulfilling existence.[17] *Instruction to the Orphic Adept*, we are advised by Dr. Stade, is one of the "truly good" poems of modern literature.[18] It is in part a translation from the Egyptian Book of the Dead, a text employed by the priests of ancient Egypt for the treatment of emotional disorders.

Professor Spears, with no demurral from Auden, had referred to the poet as "spiritual physician" and "witch-doctor."[19]

Would it be surprising if Auden had detected in Graves a disposition to play a similar role? Reviewing Graves's work, it would seem that the purport of his poetry and of his critical writing constitutes a clear-cut defense of poetry therapy. Auden's *In Memory of W. B. Yeats,* a tribute to poetry could be read as a healing modality:

> Follow poet, follow right
> To the bottom of the night,
> With your unconstraining voice
> Still persuade us to rejoice
>
> With the farming of a verse
> Make a vineyard of the curse,
> Sing of human unsuccess
> In a rapture of distress;
>
> In the deserts of the heart
> Let the healing fountain start,
> In the prison of his days
> Teach the free man how to praise.[20]

Professor Harold J. Laski of the London School of Economics, in his introduction to a reprint of John Stuart Mill's *Autobiography,* describes the book as "a document of the first importance and the most imperishable of Mill's writings."[21] A section of the story, *A Crisis in My Mental History,* covers the period 1826–1827 when Mill fell victim to a nervous disorder characterized by a state of deep depression. In this chapter the celebrated political scientist, economist, philosopher, and logician presents a careful exposition of his breakdown, his efforts at self-treatment, and the means through which he effected a cure. At the same time Mill provides us with a closely documented testimonial to the healing power of poetry.

At twenty Mill seemed to be pursuing a highly purposeful and fulfilling existence—intellectually rewarding, involved with humanitarian concerns—when all at once the bottom dropped out of his world. He continued with his normal routine, afflicted, however, by what Professor Packe terms "the fearful lassitude of accidie."[22] Mill describes his condition: "I was in a dull state of nerves, such as everybody is occasionally liable to; unsusceptible to enjoyment or pleasurable excitement; one of those moods when what is pleasure at other times becomes insipid or indifferent; I seemed to have nothing left to live for."[23]

The nature of this melancholia eluded easy diagnosis, but a fitting description could be found, as Mill later discovered, in these lines from Coleridge's ode, *Dejection*.

> A grief without a pang, void, dark and drear
> A drowsy, stifled, unimpassioned grief
> Which finds no natural outlet or relief
> In word, or sigh, or tear.[24]

Devastated by his ailment, he wished to discuss it with some other person, and found no one to whom he could turn.

His friends were fellow disciples of Jeremy Bentham, the apostle of Utilitarianism, who enshrined purposefulness and the intellect above all with little tolerance for anyone's emotional remission. Mill's mother had never given him a sense of being loved; while he respected his father, he had grown up fearing him. "My education, which was always his work, had been conducted without regard to the possibility of its ending in this result; and I saw no use in giving him the pain of thinking that his plans had failed, when failure was probably irremediable, and, at all events, beyond the power of his remedies.

"I became persuaded that my love of mankind, and of excellence for its own sake had worn out . . . In vain I sought relief from my favorite books, from which I had hitherto drawn strength and animation. I read them now without feeling"[25, 26]

He continues, "The effect of music I had often experienced; but like all my pleasurable susceptibilities it was suspended during the gloomy period. I had sought relief again and again from this quarter but found none."[27]

He believed that he had lost the capacity to feel but forced himself to carry on mechanically and purely from force of habit. "To know that a feeling would make me happy if I had it, did not give me the feeling."[28]

"At first I hoped that the cloud would pass away of itself but it did not." He turned to thoughts of release by suicide. "I frequently asked myself if I could, or if I was bound to go on living when life must be passed in this manner. I generally answered to myself that I did not think I could possibly bear it beyond a year."[29]

However, 6 months after the onset of his melancholia he chanced upon a sentimental story by a Frenchman which affected him profoundly, since it touched upon some deep-seated, possibly repressed hostility against his father.

"I was reading, accidentally, Marmontel's *Memoires* and came to the passage which relates his father's death, the distressed position of his family, and the sudden inspiration by which he, then a mere boy, felt and made them feel that he would be everything to them—would supply the place of all that they had lost. A vivid conception of the scene and its feelings came over me, and I was moved to tears. From this moment my burden grew lighter. The oppression of the thought that all feeling was dead within me was gone. I was no longer hopeless."[30]

It is to be noted that Marmontel had reached Mill not through the quality of his writing. The value of bibliotherapy in this instance was based on the special personal meaning which the scene and its characters had for Mill. The experience with this reading helped; but it was not until he opened a volume of Wordsworth's poems that he discovered a lasting cure.

His father, like other Benthamites, while concerned with the human condition, underrated poetry. As "reasoning machines,"[31] they decried "all poetry as misrepresentation."[32] Mill's father, for instance, observed of Thomas Moore, "Mr. Moore is a poet and therefore is not a reasoner."[33] As for John Stuart Mill, "The correct statement would be, not that I disliked poetry, but that I was theoretically indifferent to it . . . And I was wholly blind to its place in human culture, as a means of educating the feelings."[34]

It was in the autumn of 1828, 2 years after the first onset of his trauma, that Mill picked up a collection of Wordsworth. This happened, as he writes, "out of curiosity, with no expectation of mental relief from it."[35] Yet it was here that he discovered the clue which conducted him out of the labyrinth of hopelessness. Wordsworth, he tells us, was exactly what suited his condition.

"I had looked into the *Excursion* two or three years before and found little in it; and I should probably have found as little had I read it this time. But the miscellaneous poems, in the two-volume edition of 1815 . . . proved to be the precise thing for my mental wants at that particular juncture.

"In the first place, these poems addressed themselves powerfully to one of the strongest of my pleasurable susceptibilities, the love of rural objects and natural scenery . . . But Wordsworth would never have had any great effect upon me, if he had merely placed before me beautiful pictures of natural scenery. . . . what made Wordsworth's poems medicine for my state of mind was that they expressed not mere outward beauty, but states of feeling, and of thought colored by feeling under the excitement of beauty. . . . I needed to be made to feel that there was real, permanent happiness in tranquil contemplation. Wordsworth taught me this, not only without turning away from, but with a greatly increased interest in the common feelings and common destiny of human beings. And the delight which these poems gave me proved that with culture of this sort, there was nothing to dread from the most confirmed habit of analysis."[36]

The reassurance and emotional enrichment derived from the poet supplied answers to Mill's previous doubts regarding his emotional capacity and the value of his intellectual strivings. It also disposed of his sense of estrangement.

"At the conclusion of the *Poems* came the famous ode, *Intimations of Immortality* in which . . . I found that he too had similar experiences to mine . . . that he had sought compensation and found it in the way he was teaching me to find it. The result was that I gradually but completely emerged from my habitual depression, and was never again subject to it."[37]

John Stuart Mill spoke of Wordsworth's poetry as medicine, not simply as metaphor but in the same sense that Graves referred to a well chosen anthology of poems as "a complete dispensary for the more common mental disorders that may be used as much for prevention as for cure." Auden, in his appearance at the Downstate Medical Center, told of an unfulfilled ambition of his to serve as bishop (as did his grandfather) in the Anglican

Church. Both Cardinal Newman and John Keble, prominent cleric and professor of poetry at Oxford, wrote poetry and were (until Newman's conversion to Roman Catholicism) prelates of the same Anglican Church (with its poetic tradition, going back to John Donne, Dean of St. Paul's) where it was Auden's dream to officiate, following in the steps of his grandfather. Keble and Newman both had testified to the curative power of poetry. Cardinal Newman spoke of poetry as a means of "relieving the over-burdened minds"[38] and of affording the poet "a channel through which emotion finds expression, and that a safe, regulated expression." It accomplishes "thus a cleansing, as Aristotle would word it, of the sick soul."[39] John Keble theorized at length on poetry's therapeutic role: "Here, no doubt, is one final cause of poetry: to innumerable persons it acts as a safety valve tending to preserve them from mental disease."[40] (This view coincides closely with Auden's as recalled by Isherwood.) John Keble was in fact a proto-Freudian, anticipating in his discussion of poetry as psychotherapy much of Freud's exposition of the dynamics of repression and its pathogenic effects. Poetic form, according to Keble, provides the necessary veils and disguises that circumvent resistance to expression. By facilitating the expression of repressed emotion, the poem enables therapeutic release and assists in the resolution of the poet's conflict.

Frederick C. Prescott's study, *The Poetic Mind*, notably recognizes poetry as therapy. Professor Stanley Burnshaw, in his foreword to the 1959 reprinting of Prescott's seminal dissertation, points out that the latter "counts heavily on certain theories advanced by the Rev. John Keble. Indeed if *The Poetic Mind* was noteworthy for relating Freud to literature, it was even more remarkable for rescuing and emphasizing the radical ideas that Keble had ventured eighteen years before the birth of Freud."[41]

Keble had described literature as unconscious autobiography and disguised wish-fulfillment."[42] Prescott, accepting Keble's theories, further develops them by drawing on Freud and the testimony of a range of poets.

In line with Keble's thinking, Prescott attributes poetry's therapeutic value first as a safety valve, satisfying "what Keble calls the instinctive wish to communicate."[43] Secondly, it serves as a means of obtaining through the imagination what had been desired and denied in reality.

In respect to the first, Prescott quotes Byron: "Poetry is the lava of the imagination whose eruption prevents the earthquake. They say poets never or rarely go mad . . . but (they) are generally so near it that I cannot help thinking rhyme is so far useful in anticipating and preventing the disorder."[44]

As for the second reason that poetry secures relief, Prescott observes "For the desire, giving rise to passion, repression, and madness, the poetic vision and the poetry afford a fictional gratification which tends to ally the desire and the emotional tension. . . . A poet when his vision is over may still feel his desire, but . . . even the fictional gratification puts the desire on the way to its ultimate actual satisfaction; and at any rate is robbed of its noxious effect. To this the poets testify as we have seen. Poetry is therefore broadly a safeguard for the individual and for the race against mental disturbance and disease."[45]

Molly Harrower, professor of psychology, concludes, "Poetry is therapy. . . . The very act of creating is a self-sustaining experience, and in the poetic moment the self becomes both the ministering 'therapist' and the comforted 'patient'."[46] Keble had described poetry as a safety valve; Harrower calls it "a built-in safeguard."

Poetry and insanity represent alternate forms of self-expression; each provides a vehicle for dealing with censored feelings and interdicted desires; both are means for the management of overpowering anxieties. The hysterical imagination is indeed an insane poetic one, the distinction being that in insanity the pathological product is disordered; poetry, whatever its genesis, is essentially a controlled expression of the organism. In *Illusion and Reality, A Study of Sources of Poetry*, Christopher Caudwell observes, "Although there is a correspondence between artistic and schizophrenic solutions, . . . the goal is in fact the opposite. As compared with existing normality, the mad road leads to greater illusion, unconsciousness, and privacy, the scientific or artistic road to greater reality, consciousness and publicity."[47] The poet through his art may skirt madness while retaining his base in reality. How is the reader helped? Keble spoke of the *vis medica poetica,* the powerful medice of poetry. It is through his identification with the poet and his dilemma that the reader discovers outlet for his own repressions and inhibitions. Poetry operates as a "safe, regulated expression," as a counter-phobic for events that might have been engineered into emotional disturbance. "In the creative act we witness neither dissociation nor mere bisociation but integration and synthesis."[48]

Poetry has been referred to as the "great universal hypnotic, the all-time great mind-altering drug,"[49] and "as a healing process based on self-analysis."[50] It is adept at hypnosis and illusion; its components are frequently made up of dream, play, fantasy, and fictional gratification. A passage from Wordsworth's *Prelude* illustrates how poetry provides an essential need that reorients the reader to reality: "Dumb yearnings, hidden appetites are ours and they must have their food."[51]

The tales that charm away the wakeful night.
In Araby, romances: legends penned
For solace by dim light of monkish lamps;
Fictions, for ladies of their love, devised
By youthful squires; adventures endless, spun
By the dismantled warrior in old age
Out of the bowels of those very schemes
In which his youth did first extravagate;
These spread like day, and something in the shape
Of these will live till man shall be no more.
Dumb yearnings, hidden appetites, are ours,
And they must have their food. Our childhood sits,
Our simple childhood, sits upon a throne
That hath more power than all the elements,
I guess not what this tells of Being past,
Nor what it augurs of the life to come;
But so it is; and in that dubious hour,
That twilight—when we first begin to see
This dawning earth, to recognize, expect
And in the long probation that ensues,
The time of trial, ere we learn to live
In reconcilement with our stinted powers;
To endure this state of meagre vassalage,
Unwilling to forego, confess, submit,
Uneasy and unsettled, yoke-fellows
To custom mettlesome, and not yet tamed
And humbled down;—oh! then we feel, we feel,

We know where we have friends. Ye dreamers, then,
Forgers of daring tales! We bless you then,
Imposters, drivellers, dotards, as the ape
Philosophy will call you: then we feel
With what, and how great might ye are in league,
Who make our wish, our power, our thought a deed,
An empire, a possession[52]

Literature is a force, an act of human magic that alters the way we see our lives and so changes us. Prescott observed, "poetry in general 'cleanses the sick soul' and in its various forms should be recognized as a hygienic and curative agent of the highest value. Apollo has for his province both poetry and healing—not only the healing of the body but the more important care of the mind."[53]

As Auden told us, writing "helps us a little better to enjoy life or a little better to endure it."[54] This is the mutual function of the poet and the psychotherapist.

REFERENCES

1. *New York Times,* December 16, 1970, sec. O, p. 49.

2. Goldenson, R. M. *The encyclopedia of human behavior.* Garden City; Doubleday, 1970, II, 1082.

3. Spears, M. K. *The poetry of W. H. Auden.* Oxford; Oxford University Press, 1935, p. 62.

4. *Ibid,* p. 5.

5. Isherwood, C. Some notes on Auden's early poetry. In M. K. Spears, (Ed.), *Auden: A collection of critical essays.* Englewood Cliffs: Prentice-Hall, 1964, p. 13.

6. Spears, M. K. *The poetry of W. H. Auden.* (dustjacket).

7. *Ibid,* p. V.

8. *Ibid,* p. 7.

9. Davie, D. Remembering the movement. *Prospect,* Summer 1959, p. 16.

10. Spears, op. cit., p. 65.

11.   Stade, G. *Robert Graves*. New York: Columbia University Press, 1967, p. 9.

12.   *Ibid,* p. 42.

13.   *Ibid,* p. 11.

14.   Id.

15.   *Ibid,* p. 12.

16.   *Ibid,* p. 48.

17.   Goldenson, op cit, p. 1082.

18.   Stade, op cit, p. 42.

19.   Spears, op cit, p. 7.

20.   Auden, W. H. In memory of W. B. Yeats. In *The collected poetry of W. H. Auden.* New York: Random House, 1966, p. 143.

21.   Mill, J. S. *Autobiography.* London; Oxford University Press, 1949, pp. IX, XX.

22.   Packe, M. St. J. *The life of John Stuart Mill.* New York: Macmillan, 1954, p. 80.

23.   Mill, op cit, p. 113.

24.   *Ibid,* p. 114.

25.   *Ibid,* p. 115.

26.   *Ibid,* p. 114.

27.   *Ibid,* p. 122.

28.   *Ibid,* p. 117.

29.   *Ibid,* p. 113.

30.   *Ibid,* p. 119.

31.   *Ibid,* p. 92.

32.   *Ibid,* p. 94.

33.   *Ibid,* p. 95.

34.   Id.

35.   *Ibid,* p. 124.

36.   *Ibid,* p. 125.

37.   *Ibid,* p. 126.

38.   Prescott, F. C. *The poetic mind.* Ithaca: Cornell University Press, 1959, p. 271.

39. *Ibid,* p. 271.

40. Id.

41. *Ibid,* p. VI.

42. Id.

43. *Ibid,* p. 273.

44. *Ibid,* p. 272.

45. *Ibid,* p. 273–274.

46. Harrower, M. *The therapy of poetry.* Springfield, Ill.: Charles C. Thomas, 1972, p. 3.

47. Caudwell, C. *Illusion and reality, A study of the sources of poetry* (2nd ed.). New York: International Publishers, 1970, p. 230.

48. Barron, F. The creative personality akin to madness. *Psychology Today,* July 1972, p. 85.

49. Brandon, W. (Ed.). *The magic world, American Indian songs and poems.* New York; William Morrow, 1971, p. XI.

50. Prescott, op cit, p. 276.

51. *Ibid,* p. 275.

52. Id.

53. *Ibid,* p. 277.

54. *New York Times,* op cit, p. 49.

Chapter 3

THE IMAGE AND THE POEM

Betty Sue Flowers

Mental images, like dreams, are notoriously difficult to study. Since they can never be approached directly, one must look at them through the distorting lens of informant reports. The dreamer or reader of poetry tells us what was seen, and the telling itself obscures, exaggerates, excises, and, inevitably, shapes itself in response to the questions asked.

For example, in an informal study which W. O. S. Sutherland and I conducted, a questionnaire elicited student responses to the reading of W. C. Williams's *The Red Wheelbarrow:*[1]

> so much depends
> upon
>
> a red wheel
> barrow
>
> glazed with rain
> water
>
> beside the white
> chickens.

We noticed that if we asked a question in such a way as to elicit a "yes" or "no" answer, the responses could be quantified, made "objective." For example, if we asked, "In reading *The Red Wheelbarrow* do you have an image of chickens?"—almost everyone answered "yes." But by asking even a slightly more open-ended question—"Where are they?"—we see that the uniform "yes" to the previous question masks a wide diversity of mental experience.

Even the relatively open question, "Where are they?" seems to call for one of only four answers: in front, behind, to the left, or to the right of the wheelbarrow. However, in a class of 16, we found only one repeated response. Other answers ranged from "Around the yard where the wheelbarrow is located," to "in the cage," to "in the yard around the chicken house and some in the chicken house," to "on the edge, precariously taking a drink of water," to "behind the white fence and they can't get out."

The "white fence"—along with chicken coops, barns, farmhouses, farm tools, stray tennis shoes, and many other objects not specifically mentioned by the poet—suggests that readers tend to *add* something to the poem. In most cases, though, the additions could be described as the fleshing out of scenes, rather than as independent creations. Visual images are complemented by auditory images (the cackle and clucking of hens), olfactory images (the smell of fertile earth, spring smells, the stink of a chicken coop), and, in many instances, the dynamic movement of the objects seen. Some readers report the scene to occur in spring, some autumn. For one it is evening, for another dusk. There are reports of its raining and of its not raining. One reader even reports *two* wheelbarrows!

This definiteness of statement seems to be part of a strong tendency to create a consistent, rational scene for the poem. Almost every reader sees some sort of place—farmyard, farmhouse, chickenyard—and even those who are not so specific mention images such as a dirt road, a picket fence, a sidewalk, or green grass.

Within this setting, the images are very often tied together, both visually and narratively. One reader imagines a picket fence; the chickens are behind it with the wheelbarrow in front, the fence making a notable visual addition. Another reader, after mentioning "the farm" and "the mud" adds, "Maybe a tennis shoe left from the kids who were playing before it started raining." This reader has made a story for the poem to be taken from. Some readers mention that the wheelbarrow has water in it for the chickens to drink. Wheelbarrow, rain water, chickens—all the major elements of the poem—thus come together for an obvious, rational purpose.

Often the unifying scene or image seems to be constructed to answer questions raised implicitly by the visual element of the poem. Why is the wheelbarrow there? What has the rain water to do with the scene? How do the chickens fit in? No one answers such questions consciously—at least in their reports—but the questions are often answered very clearly in the images reported. And sometimes readers supplement these images by explaining why they are there.

Remembered imagery, even if it later is seen to contradict the written text, seems to exert a powerful influence on responses to the questionnaire. One reader, asked what he remembered of the poem several weeks later, said he was "confused," and that all he could remember was "separate pieces, e.g., wheelbarrow, rain, chick, all trying to fit some pattern." Later, given the questionnaire, with the text of the poem and its plural "chickens" clearly in view, the reader said, "I picture a very rainy day. The rain is beating down hard on a very shiny red light-weight wheelbarrow. The white chicken is running around aimlessly." On the second page of the questionnaire, however, when asked, "How many chickens?" he responded, "5 to 6." And later in the semester, when asked what he remembered of the poem, he reported, "a farm scene with white chickens running around." The "running around" remains the same, but the number of chickens has been corrected.

This remembered imagery seems to be highly resistant to correction. For the surprisingly large number of students who saw a red wagon rather than a red wheelbarrow, the change to wheelbarrow was not an easy one to make. Many reported the wagon as a childhood memory; the scene evoked in response to the poem was often, then, a scene from childhood which included the remembered image of a red wagon. When we again gave the students a copy of the poem, many readers changed "wagon" to "wheelbarrow." But the stability of this change is called into question by remarks such as those of a student who wrote, "I realized somewhere in here, the image of the wheelbarrow changed in my mind to the image of a wagon." Later she added: "All throughout, my image is of a wagon vs. a wheelbarrow. I realized it later." Another reader reported that his image was based upon "my own wheelbarrow that I had at one time"; but in one description, he used the word "wagon" rather than "wheelbarrow," raising the question of whether even in using the word "wheelbarrow" he was not actually imagining a wagon. Two readers out of 16, while responding to the questionnaire in terms of "wheelbarrow," when asked at the end of the semester what they remembered of the W. C. Williams poem we had read, responded, "red wagon." "If I can recall correctly," said one reader, "the poem you are referring to was *The Little Red Wagon*. I remember seeing a bright red wagon sitting on a very green lawn with a white chicken beside the wagon."

In addition to discovering that mental images were often resistant to change, we also found that the kinds of images and the connections among them which readers report are related to the kinds of interpretations of the poems they give. One reader, for example, who takes an essentially aesthetic point of view toward *The Red Wheelbarrow,* writes:

> From reading the poem I have a visual image which is bright and vivid. Defined colors: bright red wheelbarrow, shining with water, lying on its side on shining green grass. There are several clean, white chickens milling around next to it.

When asked in what sense anything depended on the wheelbarrow, she says:

> That's the hardest to explain. The image is not the poem, it's the first line—because it could be followed by any image. Anything could depend on something as seemingly minute as a glance at a wheelbarrow.

But another reader sees the scene in much more utilitarian

images. Having noted the object of the poem, he adds from his own imagination:

> more details of the farm setting. Fences, water troughs,
> open field in the background. Two or three trees in the
> area where the barrow is and a feed shack possibly.

When asked in what sense did anything depend on the wheelbarrow, he replies:

> . . . work. Hauling cans of feed from one trough to an-
> other, etc.

In both cases, and in those which are like them, the image seems to have been in the reader's consciousness prior to any explanation in words. What, then, is the relation of interpretation to the origin of imagery? Where do images come from? Is there a particular period of childhood which provides visual memories which we use to respond to poems? Does the source of imagery vary with age? Is there any relation between the source of imagery and how well a reader likes a poem? A good deal of evidence would be required before any sort of definitive statement could be made in response to such questions.

In administering the questionnaire to more than 100 students, we did notice two characteristics—consistency and diversity—which might have a direct bearing on the use of mental images and healing. Mental images, even those which are "mistaken" in relation to the poem, tend to remain consistent over time. Perhaps one reason for this is their linkage to emotions and attitudes, both of which are also resistant to change, in part because they are so often unconscious. Changing an image may be one way to work toward changing an attitude or emotion. For example, a child afraid of a shadowy "bear" in the corner of his room at night might not respond to the admonition not to be afraid. However, if he is taught to change his image, to see the shadow as a lamp or a chair, there is a greater likelihood that the emotion might change, too. Similarly, an adult who realizes that the image she carries of her boss is that of a 7-foot-tall police officer might practice envisioning him as a first grader in order to "bring him down to size." Dreams often perform this compensatory function by offering absurd images of authority figures or by enhancing the images of those whom we have undervalued—including ourselves.

The second important characteristic we observed was the diversity of responses. When we discussed the results of the questionnaire in classes, students often expressed amazement at this diversity. One student said that while he *knew* intellectually that there were other ways to see the images in the poem, he couldn't help *feeling* that what he saw was the correct response to what the poem was saying. Becoming aware of the diversity of possible responses to a situation, whether the reading of the poem or a difficult encounter with a loved one, allows us to exercise the freedom which we have but which we may forget—including the freedom to try other responses, to change our behavior. In addition, students' amazement at the diversity of responses was followed by appreciation of that diversity—and appreciation of diversity is a key to the tolerance which promotes healing among groups as well as within individuals.

REFERENCE

1. Williams, W. C. The red wheelbarrow. In *Collected earlier poems*. New York: New Directions Publishing Corp., 1938.

Chapter 4

WHERE DO IMAGES COME FROM?

William Sutherland

Dr. Flowers's chapter describes our project and suggests the remarkable diversity we have found in the images with which our subjects respond to the reading of a poetic text. We feel that what we are learning has a number of implications. One, arising from the provenance or origin of the image, seems especially important and is the subject of this chapter. Where do readers' images come from? What does understanding the provenance tell us about the images readers have?

Most of our subjects have been students from the freshman through the senior years. We plan to look at other age groups, but the results reported here are limited to that group.

First, as one might suspect, not everyone either remembers or perhaps wants to say where particular images come from. We find that among our subjects about a third are actually able to state the provenance of a particular image. At present it is difficult to say whether that is a low, normal, or high percentage. The safe conclusion is that a sizable percentage of our subjects had a stock of images vivid or memorable enough for them to place. For a large number of subjects to remember where an image of an object as common as a wheelbarrow comes from means that certain experiences remain vivid in the mind, ready to respond upon the proper stimulus. (Let me add that not all images are of common objects and that not all our friends and neighbors have undergone the common experiences of life. In such cases the images must come from elsewhere, perhaps a photograph, a construct, or some other source.) Most of our respondents reported that the sources of the images they could recall came from the period of childhood between the ages of about five and twelve. One might expect that a student nineteen or twenty would not readily recall an experience of 15 years ago. We might reasonably expect that older images would be overlain by newer ones, but that does not seem to be the way we function. This may tell us that college students (the only group for which we can now draw that conclusion) live in a world that in part is populated by images of childhood and adolescence. We know, of course, how important the early years are; yet may often fail to understand or consider their importance for the creation of mental imagery. As observed by Louis McNeice, what we are working toward is understanding what past experience means to us in the present. Reading is also apparently a kind of recalling. We are reading in the present in terms of the experiences we had in the past, sometimes the rather distant past. Images, of course, are not the only ways we process information or think or remember. They are but one part of that process. But it gives pause to realize that even in reading sophisticated poetic texts, students are going back to images that they did not experience in their more mature years.

These images may carry with them heavy emotional baggage. The student who upon reading *The Red Wheelbarrow* looks sadly through the pane of glass at the wheelbarrow in the rain may be remembering a farm and the emotions she felt at some time on a visit to that farm. That is a very strong predisposition. There is nothing inherently sad about *The Red Wheelbarrow*. However, through our work with images we can to some extent identify that particular student's predisposition; without the image neither we nor the student would even be aware that the predisposition existed. In class we would say to the student, "Point out in the text what makes you think this poem is sad." This of course the student cannot. It is not in the text. We face one another baffled.

Of course, all images do not come from childhood. Some come from recent experiences. One student reported on a passage from Mary Shelley's novel *Frankenstein*. The setting is Switzerland and Frankenstein meets the creature on the glacier on Mont Blanc. Since few of the students had been to Mont Blanc (one had) it was interesting how they would read this passage, especially through what images. Everyone responded with an image, though not many remembered where it came from. One student remembered the source, even with great pleasure. The year before he had been on a winter camping trip into the Colorado Rockies near Aspen. He remembered standing on the side of the mountain looking out over the snow-covered hills and valleys; this was the setting for the meeting of Frankenstein and his creation. Another student reported that his image of Mont Blanc came from a cartoon he had seen named *Rin Tin Tin in Tibet*. The point to be made is that both reports were inappropriate to the text being read. Both students knew this; but it didn't seem to make any difference. So far as they were concerned, the image "worked." But of course they were not making a conscious choice; it seems apparent that these images are involuntary, that we are not able to exercise any conscious censorship or discrimination. Does that mean we have to stay with the first image that arises? Obviously, with these students, it did.

This is a disturbing phenomenon, for it means that at least some of the experience we call up is used in an irrational way. In Robert Frost's poem *Stopping by Woods on a Snowy Evening*, a student reported that the scene of falling snow is illuminated by the light of the moon. Frost fixes the setting as "the darkest evening of the year."

The student who found his glacier outside Aspen, Colorado, was using his own experience, and certainly our personal experience has a very clear effect on the way we read. We drag our experience into the text whether it fits the poem or not. In the same poem by Frost the speaker stops his horse (who "gives his harness bells a shake") and watches the snow fall in the woods. "Whose woods these are I do not know,/ His house is in the village though. . . ." One colleague upon hearing that a student had reported the poet was on *horseback* smiled and said, "Of course, he was in a *sleigh*." The text does not specify. One colleague, hearing about "the moon" shining, said, "I had always thought the light came from the nearby village." Both these remarks make "sense"; but both are metatextual.

We might well ask, if we are mistaken in our impression and discover that we are, why we don't correct it, or at least abandon what is misleading. The answer is complex.We do modify and change our images as we follow along in a text. William Stafford's poem *Traveling Through the Dark* begins with traveling along the Wilson River Road. The setting is developed; then it turns out that it is night, and there is a red glow from the tail-lights. At the end, though you might have suspected this from the start, it turns out that there is a deep canyon by the road. None of this is surprising to the reader, but it does require some adjustment in the image. So far as we can tell, that sort of change is accomplished with no difficulty. But the reader is led by the poet.

Another group of students read Wordsworth's poem *Composed upon Westminster Bridge*, wrote their impressions, and discussed them, most freely and cooperatively. (This is the usual response: people have never been asked about their images before, and most of them have a lot to say. Perhaps there is some relief in finding out this is a common human trait, and not an aberration.)

After we had talked about our images and the poem, a sheet was passed out which acknowledged in effect that they had reported their reading. Now, they were asked, read through the poem again *changing your image as completely as you can.* This would seem an interesting, not unreasonable request, but, in Alexander Pope's line, "No applause ensued." The class became restless; one student said "Do we *have* to?" A tangible pall fell over the group, and the resultant responses were brief and apparently rather perfunctory. That group *resisted* the request. They wanted to stay with their first images: even the girl who had used a sketch of New York Harbor in the nineteenth century as the basis for her image.

Here we may touch on something very interesting, perhaps even disturbing. It comes to mind that when people discuss their images, never does one say, "I like *your* image. I think I'll use it instead of the one I had." Though images may arise out of childhood, though they may be erroneous, they exert "staying power."

It may be a poor thing, but it's *mine.* This is an area where further work is needed. There must be ways to change images painlessly, through paintings and photographs or something that seems authentic or historical. (Indeed, the advertising agencies may have been there before us.) This technique would be especially useful in teaching history and literature from earlier periods. What did a Texas cowboy in the 1880s look like? How did Jane Austen's characters, or Antigone, or Hamlet dress?

Our experience certainly includes content other than what we have personally experienced. Illustrations furnish sources for images too; students turn to them especially for images out of their immediate ken, massive snow and ice, for example. Currier and Ives prints and the *National Geographic Magazine* are two examples. Television is not, as might have been expected, mentioned as a source.

In all this we seem to have found one way to trace how our experience affects our thought processes and our attitudes. We know that a number of those experiences come in childhood and adolescence and that they seem to remain unchanged over years. What this means to an individual will depend upon his particular area of interest and how useful such a technique can be. For teachers it tells a good deal about ways of teaching and ways of understanding how students arrive at their interpretations of literature. It especially shows how often teachers unconsciously impose their own images on students and how important it is to let students use their own experience.

People live in two worlds: the sensory world of the present, and the world of recalled images. Neither is that mental world one of our own choosing. In a sense we live by reliving. We make sense of the present by using the past. If we cannot bring them together, we lack mental health, the ability to use our experience. If we can, we are able to use the past, for understanding comes out of the melding of the two.

Chapter 5

VOICES FROM WITHIN THE PROCESS

Of Writing and Reminiscing in Old Age*

Marc Kaminsky

Poetry, according to Coleridge, brings the whole soul of the poet into activity. Wallace Stevens repealed the *soul* and repeated the dictum for modern readers: "Poetry is part of the process of the poet's personality." Writing, a writer might say, "feels like everything"—part of the world with which one makes contact; part of the self in its moments of wholeness, a feeling, and a means of integration. For a writer, writing is a generative, a creative act: the word becomes flesh—not an artifact, but a living thing. Whitman's "leaves of grass," for instance, are the poems on the page; his innermost, departing thoughts ("the frailest leaves of me"), as he stands before us for the thousandth time, saying good-bye; his fragrant physicality ("the scented herbiage of my breast"); the green surface of the earth, which is a sacrament, being "God's handkerchief"; the title of the book he worked on all his life; his fate, as it is everyone's fate, for Whitman

*Previously published in *Gerontological Social Work in the Community*, edited by G. Gertzel & J. Mellor. Haworth Press, New York, 1984. Used by permission of publisher.

was continually aware that "all flesh is grass." Perhaps more boldly than anyone before or since, he confessed what poets feel when he said, if not in these words, "Take this book; it is my body."

Critics may "deconstruct" the presence of the writer, so that they can possess the pure body of the text. They may deflate the imagination which bestows being on syllables. But no poem could be written, no art made, without faith in a resurrection, in a "second life of art": Eugenio Montale's faith that the value of a work of art lies in its unpredictable and "obscure pilgrimage through the conscience and memory of men, its entire flowing back into the very life from which art itself took its first nourishment ... A fragment of music or poetry, a page, a picture begins to live in the act of their creation but they complete their existence when they circulate ... Paradoxically, one could say that (they) begin to be understood when they are presented, but they do not truly live if they lack the capacity to continue to exercise their powers beyond that moment, freeing themselves, mirroring themselves in that particular situation of life which made them possible. To enjoy a work of art or its moment, in short, is to discover it outside its context; only in that instant does the circle of understanding close and art becomes one with life as all the romantics dreamed."[1]

For a writer, the letter giveth life; periods of not writing are little deaths. And so when a person of Coleridge's faith—and Whitman's and Steven's and Montale's and that of any true poet—enters the workshop, he may never need to teach the most fundamental thing that he has to impart: his feeling that writing is a life-giving act. It is in the atmosphere that he carries around him; it is a kind of spiritual axiom upon which the development of talent depends. And isn't it natural that the faith of such a person would have special value for people whose old age comes in an age of shattered faiths?

Writing, for a writer, is not therapy: it is life. And a vision of life; in our century, a violent, death-haunted vision. "The important thing," said Camus, "is not to be cured, but to live with one's afflictions." By writing, the writer bears what he knows, and sees, and suffers, and *is*. There is no "cure." We live in the century that reveals its character most by its inventiveness in terrorizing and murdering vast populations. Existence, as in other dark times, feels precarious. For us, art is no longer a refuge.

Poets may go on seeing beauty, as before, but it is likely to be the "terrible beauty" that Yeats found in *Easter, 1916*. Rilke, in the first lines of the *Duino Elegies*, discovers that "beauty is nothing but the beginning of terror we're still just able to bear."[2] James Wright, watching a high-school football game, sees American boys grow "suicidally beautiful" as they "gallop terribly against each other's bodies."[3] Those old people whom we account wise know that the intensity of life we yearn for may arise out of self-destructiveness, and that no good can come of denying paradox, chance,and evil. They know there is no cure: we're imperfect, we're guilty, and we die. And they welcome a vision of things adequate to their knowledge.

If they distrust poetry, it is because they have been taught that poetry shows us nothing but the land of our heart's desire. But the imagination constructs its pleasure domes or Sunday mornings, its open roads or Byzantiums so that it may have a place apart, on which to stand, beyond the reach of "the average expectable environment"; and there it looks out upon things as they are and sees what cannot be seen if one doesn't have what Virginia Woolf called "a station in midair." The imagination is not to be dismissed because it is a light and floating thing: without it, poets couldn't rise above narrow circumstances and reconnoiter the real.

The writer, upon entering the workshop, hopes to teach people to write as writers do: out of the pressure of life upon the imagination, out of necessity. It is useful, even pleasurable, to teach grammar, prosody, the secret paths of metaphor; but it is necessary to bring the whole soul into activity.

And this takes time, and repeated attempts to capture a feeling or a peculiar slant of that lies just beyond the reach of the words we've learned to deploy. Six or ten sessions won't do it. But given time—say a year or two—the writer is able to impart the experience that corresponds to the faith of poets. The people in the workshop come to discover that writing is neither a single activity nor a single process. It comprehends dreaming and observing, spontaneity and calculation, intuition and skill; it elicits, energizes, gives form and direction to the "buzzing, blooming confusion" (William James) of thoughts, memories, feelings, and perceptions that pulse through the mind in odd clusters, glimmering for a moment—then they're gone. Writing redeems them.

It salvages odd scraps of experience. It transforms receptivity into activity, loneliness into solitude; silence becomes part of a dialogue with a *thou* whose absence or presence awakens new powers of speech.

And the writer listens to what the people in the workshop say. The feelings which their voices manifest enable him to feel meaning in the workshop. Later, their voices return to him, like a musical phrase or a line in a poem that comes back to liberate what is really going on—and is marvelous—from its routine appearance. He can no longer talk about the writing workshop without calling on them, for their individual voices have become part of his understanding of what the workshop means. When he arranges their voices into an abstract order, a kind of chorus that sums things up, he hears them affirm that the workshop brings into play a wide range of emotional and intellectual processes that have adaptive value in old age. That's a way of putting it, but their individual voices speak more powerfully, more memorably, than the collective affirmation they make. Listen! They return to speak about writing, about reminiscing and aging, about being in an art-making workshop; they are saying it enables them—

1. *To continue learning:*

"It was very hesitant in the beginning. School to me—when I was growing up in Germany—was like a military school, discipline and listening. And when we started with grammar here in the group, I really wanted to run away. I was really afraid. I cannot write rhymes, and grammar to learn at this age was for me horrifying. But I must say I learned a lot, and it was not the school type that I thought it would be. It's a very relaxed group, and when I do one bad work the next one is a little better, and I don't feel I'm a failure. In the beginning I was very much afraid I could not go with a group in English. I was afraid of my mistakes, and it all worked out so beautifully that no one cares if I make mistakes. I write what I feel like. I have learned quite a lot."*

—Irene Salamon, Astoria Workshop**

**Four senior centers conducted under the auspices of JASA (the Jewish Association for Services for the Aged) were the sites of the writing workshops whose participants are quoted in this piece.

"I was asked to join the writing workshop, and I didn't want to. I do love English, but I was upset about the word 'poetry.' I can't rhyme, and I didn't want to start something that I already had a feeling I wouldn't like. However, I became very interested, was also a little argumentative, I'd forgotten that poetry doesn't always have to rhyme. I was completely bewildered by the first poem the writer brought in. I couldn't get anything out of it, and it was English, it was simple, short, and then we took his attitude and so many things came out of every word! He's very analytical, but it's like an injection that you get; they give it to you directly in your blood because it's the fastest way to get to you. It just has to go into your blood, a little goes here, a little goes there; and you hear, see, and then you look at the poem and you understand it; but at the beginning it's nothing, and that is the way other things are. Once he gave us an assignment about color, and I thought: Now what can I write about color? Now I don't say that every time I wrote something it was what I would have liked to have done, or as well, but I saw something that I didn't see before. And as it came to me, the words, a little window was opened to me. It's hard for me to describe in words. I see a little clearer, I hear a little clearer perhaps, and not only as far as poetry is concerned. As I say, he injected the words, I don't mean it's painful, he opens up a little window, and it's better than no window. Once at three o'clock in the morning, I wrote a poem, a poet I may never be, but I am a little window. It all came to me.

"I look at poetry different now—it's clearer, it's closer to me. I don't know if I can enjoy reading heavy poetry much better than before, but I read it, I feel it differently. It's satisfying. I feel I've learned. It's late in life, but I seem to be able to learn, I think, from every little contact that I have."*

—Aurelia Goldin, Astoria Workshop

2. *To draw upon unused skills, experience, knowledge; to put themselves to use; to make full use of their powers:*

"I joined the writing workshop to stimulate my mind once

---

*Quotations followed by an asterisk are from an interview of the Astoria Workshop by Janet Bloom. See "A Window was Opened to Me," *Teachers & Writers Magazine*, Fall 1980, *12*(1), pp. 12–14.

again. I felt that I was stagnating. My other interests were emotionally fulfilling but not necessarily mentally fulfilling. I needed another source of challenge."

—Bea Lipsett, Astoria Workshop

"Now that I'm no longer committed to a job, I find it necessary to do something to keep my mind working. As you're growing up, you have to go to school. Then when you get married, you have a family, then you have certain responsibilities. Then when you go to work, you have your family, and your work, and your responsibilities, and sometimes it gets to the point where it feels like it's choking you. And so, when you stop working, and your family is grown, and you don't have to worry about them anymore, then you feel: 'Well, gee, now this is time for me.' Which is something that you couldn't do before because if you have an infant it has to be washed and fed and dressed; as the kids get older you have to take them to school and bring them back and forth. And so this is the time of your life when you can say: 'The hell with everything and everybody, now I can take care of me, and I can do as I please and the way I please.'

"I never liked routine. I always fought against it, even as a kid. They said, 'You have to eat at twelve o'clock.' If I'm not hungry at twelve, I didn't want to eat, and this caused problems. But this class, I made it my business to miss as little as possible, because I really enjoy it very, very much and got a lot out of it. So this is what happens with most of us—you become sort of a free spirit that you don't have to worry for everything, and it's primarily yourself you're taking care of, body and soul."

—Margaret Friedman, Astoria Workshop

3. *To return to a "road not taken"; to resume an interest of their youths; to fulfill an abandoned ambition:*

"I am interested in the arts, was a millinery designer. I went to City College night classes, studied sketching and designing; later on—many years later—I studied Oriental Brushwork at the Y.M.C.A. And now the greater desire I've had I am fulfilling with this writer's group. I find I now have the ability to write my thoughts and give vent to my innermost feelings and to write with confidence."

—Millie Goemann, Rochdale Village Workshop

In *Silences,* Tillie Olsen speaks of those who could not fulfill "the greater desire," of "the silence where the lives never came to the writing. Among these, the mute inglorious Miltons: those whose waking hours were all struggle for existence; the barely educated; the illiterate; women. Their silence the silence of centuries as to how life was, is, for most of humanity."[4] The writing workshop allows their lives "to come to the writing"; allows us to hear the testimony of the silent ones: the songs, tales, superstitions, life wisdom of the furriers, "operators by blouses," survivors of two World Wars, the housewives, ordinary working women, ordinary working men, the many remarkable people among them.

"The most important regret I have—but rather I will call it negligence—is that I did not go on to college. While in high school, my plans were to become a teacher and once I was able to take care of myself financially to continue on with the study of journalism. I had always wanted to write and felt by doing it this way I would not have to depend on my parents. But many times, plans do not work out.

"I finished high school at the height of the Depression. Conditions were very bad, and I decided to go to work for a while to make it easier for my parents. They urged me to continue with school, we would be able to manage, but no, I wanted to do my share.

"Some of my friends, who were in the same situation, decided we ought to do something political in order to help shape a better world. When people were evicted for nonpayment of rent, we helped put their belongings back into their apartments. We picketed for people to get what they called 'home relief' in those days. Maybe the little we did helped. I like to think so. But all this activity kept me from going back to school.

"It still would have been possible but it was neglect on my part and I can only blame myself. It is good for youth to plan and dream because without their dreams and plans some of the wonderful books, works of art and scientific discoveries would not have happened."

—Margaret Friedman

4. *To satisfy their need for continued accomplishment; to create a "finished product" which satisfies their desire for beauty and truth and*

which has value in their eyes and in the eyes of others; to affirm themselves as creators, makers, workers:

"I wish, I wish, I wish I was a painter and could put on canvas what I see looking through my window. An autumn scene with bare trees, a light dusting of snow on dry grass. A seemingly grim, desolate picture. But as I lift my eyes skyward, I perceive dark gray-black clouds drifting from the northwest with patches of blue here and there. The near setting sun, peeking out now and then, is casting a light pink glow all around the horizon. The red brick massive buildings serve as a contrast to the multicolored panorama. The electric lights look like sparkling ornaments.

"One hour later, a complete change of scenery. The electric lights sparkle like jewels while the afterglow of the sunset is a deeper pink with gray topping. I wish, I wish I was a painter and could express my elation and excitement perceiving all this!"
—Norman Hofferman, Rochdale Village Workshop

"What does a picture of a face mean to you? 'Choose a picture of a face and write a poem or story about the face.' Within 15 minutes each of the women in our workshop showed the picture she had chosen and read what she had written.

"What imaginations! What a delightful time I had, watching and listening to the enthusiasm the women felt and expressed.

"When we were given this assignment, I felt it would be dull and uninteresting, and now I hope I can find the words to do it justice.

"Seven women were present at this session. As our writing teacher entered the room, the women were all looking at pictures brought in by Julia Schubert, who told us: 'All my life I wanted to identify with something beautiful. When I was twelve and fourteen years old, I wanted to be an artist. At that time there was a newspaper in circulation called the *Journal American*. A woman artist by the name of Nell Brinkley made drawings of the faces of pretty women, which were printed in the paper. Each day, after school, I sat with that newspaper in front of me and made pencil drawings of some of her faces. Times were hard, there was no money for drawing paper, crayons or paints. My material was the butcher's paper that was used to wrap meat. It had a certain gloss to it that I liked.' And here, many years later, were the drawings on butcher paper! Everyone commented that it was a shame Julia hadn't been able to pursue an artist's career, they were so good.

"When the writer looked at the picture and heard Julia's story, he immediately gave us the assignment.

"After the last woman read her piece, he said, 'Now look again at the picture you chose and write another piece. If you wrote a poem the first time, now write a story, and take a different point of view. If you spoke in the voice of the woman's daughter, now be her sister or her jilted lover. Or is she the one who's been jilted?'

"We wrote new pieces. Then each of the women, in turn, read her work. Following each piece, we were asked for our comments. The encouragement, empathy, and understanding shown me made me feel it was a joy to be able to do with words what Julia does with lines and shadows.

"These pieces were written in a short period of time with no preparation. The ideas expressed and imagination used made me aware that people, like wine, become more flavorful with age."

—Phene Dreher, Astoria Workshop

5. *To communicate with themselves; to explore their inner worlds through writing, through conversing with themselves apart from the presence of an intrusive audience; to turn their loneliness into solitude; to become more aware of their feelings, reveries, dreams; to have an outlet for socially unacceptable feelings of grief, loneliness, frustration, pain, rage:*

"Here I am once again. So many things come out of my mind. Tonight I want to write about that. I was just thinking of my late husband. I had a dream about him and he was talking to me just like he was alive. When I wake up, I think: this is only a dream, but it was so real. He told me, 'Don't worry too much. I am next to you, and nothing is happening to you, and such a thing comes from the mind. 'Go ahead,' he told me, 'go ahead. You have to live. I am in the next world and it's a beautiful place to stay. Some day you will come, and we will be together.'

"I accepted that for a while. But my mind is only on him. Maybe some day will come when I won't think too much of this tragedy and my thoughts and my mind will give me a different way to go. Now there is nothing important for me. I refuse to have some time for myself or to go out to a movie or other places. I don't feel in that mood. Of course, in two months it's too early, and I can't forget now this occupies all my time. If I have to do something like shopping, and if I am in a bus or subway, I am thinking of him. No other thing lets me think of other pleasures because my mind and thoughts are only on him.

"My children talk to me very often and tell me, 'Mommy, you are alive, and you have to keep going.' It's the truth. But not for now. Some day I know I want to do things in my way. I love to travel and go places and have good times like other people like to do. I know that will come to me in the future. I don't know when, but I know it will happen for sure if I don't depart soon, and nobody knows when this will happen. I am in God's hands.

"Today I was with my son, Charlie. We went to the cemetery to see his grave. The stone has to be put up, and we were going to different places, comparing prices, and everything was very expensive. But for sure I have to put the stone on his grave. There has to be a place next to him in the same place where we have to be together, resting in peace, and forever. This is so sad to say, but it's part of my life, and I have to write all the things that happen in my life, bad and good too. It happens to everybody."

—Margot Rodriguez, East Concourse Workshop

6. *To communicate with others; to overcome their loneliness by making contact with people who have suffered similar losses, known kindred feelings, struggled with comparable dilemmas; to discover a sense of generational solidarity; to be an active participant in an intimate group:*

"I notice because the group is small the people in the group have become quite friendly. It isn't just hello. They really come over and talk. I am not the only one who feels this way. Some of the members of the group say they have opened up more now. I believe that this group has helped many people. It gives you a purpose for coming to the Center and you look forward to it. I believe that most of us live alone and that is why it is important to have a purpose and to be able to express yourself."

—Anne Sager, Astoria Workshop

"Self-affirmation should not be thought of as an isolated preoccupation with my individual personality. At just the moment of feeling 'dated' I can realize that others my age feel dated too, and so, in a moment of feeling estranged from my own time, the time-now-past, I discover an unsuspected solidarity, a kinship with others of my own age. They are all peers, my age-mates, the people of 'my generation.' They are my beings in a sense that is impossible to escape. Before I even know their names, we share a secret in common. And when we meet and question each other to find a link in our common time-now-past, we already know the link must be there. They are people of my generation, and this kinship is what we share in common. This insight is the discovery of what Ortega y Gasset calls the 'concept of the generation,' a realization that I belong, unavoidably, to a particular community of human beings who have flourished at a particular time and place."

—Harry Moody, *Reflections on the Living History Project*[5]

"To me personally, it opened a whole new world. I could never talk about the past. I opened to it more than I ever thought would be possible, and it feels easy. I can talk in a way I couldn't do even with my own family many times. Yes, here I talk over things I would never have believed it possible to talk about. When I joined the group, I felt I'm the only concentration camp survivor. I felt a patronizing feeling-sorry for me in the group, and I really hated that, but I must say it was all in my mind. Maybe the first few times they wanted to be friendly with me and I didn't accept it, but right now I must say it's the greatest friendship I ever had, and I never had close friends before that I have now. I call them my friends."

—Irene Salamon

"Our center is ethnically and racially mixed. This made for strained relationships and subtle hostilities. As a result of the writing workshop, communication has opened, attitudes are changing, and center members have developed greater respect for each other. Racial attitudes have improved—people have found they have common bonds."

—Jane Rosenson, Director, JASA East Concourse Luncheon Club

"It's not only that we write, but we have a chance to discuss. It's drawn most of us out. I mean many times there were topics that we would ordinarily not talk about, but here somehow there is a feeling of real friendship. We don't seem to feel that we have to hold back; we can be really honest with one another. And I think this is a very, very important thing because I have a daughter who seems to feel that people of our generation are not as open with one another as the younger people are today. And with this particular group I find that we do have that open line of communication."

—Margaret Friedman

7. *To become more observant of what is going on in their daily lives, which they often find "empty"; and because they are writing of their immediate world, to become more actively interested in the present and to find it enriched:*

"Right now I am sitting at my very large window, thankfully not aware of anything in the future. I'm looking at what is going on outside, aware that I'm supposed to be an artist, yet not seeing what is in front of me, not realizing that all around me is beauty. I don't have to look elsewhere. I have a complete view of the sky, bright or gray, the horizon, trees, gardens, and a tremendous plane coming in for a landing, life, people walking, riding bikes, and everything that could enhance the beautiful painting. Yet up till now it was just my window that I have to clean, and I hated it for being so large, therefore saw nothing else. Right now I think: as soon as I'm able to use my arm properly and nothing's cluttering my mind, I will do what I can with what I see now."

—Millie Goemann

Streetcorner Market

Sidewalk fruit and vegetables
Arranged in colorful trays:
Red, purple, green, and yellow,
Each bright color alive:
Nature's paint, an artist's palette.

Fat red-cheeked tomatoes
Look up with laughing puffed faces.

Handfuls of dark red cherries
Send up feelers for tasting
Next to clusters of ripe purple grapes.

Yellow bananas, purple eggplants,
Lemons and oranges, red and green apples,
Lettuce and string beans, all shades of green
Brighten the city around us—
Paris on drab New York streets.

—Israel Raphael
Astoria Workshop

September 17

Right now I am aware of a beautiful Sunday afternoon.
I am aware of the vegetable garden of Rochdale
Village. The spinach I seeded a week ago already shows
the first green leaves.
Right now I am aware of a grasshopper carrying its
young on his or her back, and right now I am aware that I
never saw this before.

—Martha Rosenfelder
Rochdale Village Workshop

8. *To master potentially overwhelming experience; to come into con-*
trol of anxieties about failing physical and intellectual capacities; to find
meaning in suffering by writing narratives which make a causal con-
nection between a "bad" experience and a "good" that came out of it; to
order and clarify chaotic feelings in poems; and by adequate articulation
of thoughts and feelings that usually elude or disorganize the conscious
mind, to gain renewed assurance in one's power to understand, express,
and "make" one's own life:

"This morning I woke up thinking about the month of September when I wasn't able to walk. I called up my daughter and
asked her to come and see what she could do for me, but she
was sick herself. After talking to my daughter, a friend called,
and from my voice she asked, 'What's wrong? You sound like
you've been crying.'

"I said to her, 'I'm so hungry and I can't walk.' I had money and food in the house, but could not get to it. In less than an hour, my friend took a cab and was at my house. It took me twenty minutes to get out of bed and crawl to the door, but I made it. She then called my daughter that lives in Jersey. And when she arrived, my friend had cooked enough food to last a couple of days. My daughter from Jersey called my son whom I haven't seen since my brother's death in April, and he came right away. From September up to today, he's at my house every evening with me for a couple of hours. I now cook every day and enjoy a meal with him. I didn't enjoy being sick, but some good came of it."

—Ruth Carter, East Concourse Workshop

"I have to fight hard, as I am living alone and my children live far away. I know I cannot be ill, as I will be a burden to my children, and they sure would want to care for me. They have families of their own, and although they have wonderful children, I am sure they have their own problems to solve. I thank God every day as at this writing I am still very alert. I have wonderful children and grandchildren, and to tell you the truth I am living for them, and I cannot afford to be mentally ill at this time."

—Sarah Reiger, East Concourse Workshop

Growing Old

Growing old is like a new shoe that loses its shape from
    too many wearings
Like a new penny that loses its lustre from too many handlings
Or like an old piano that needs tuning up more often

—*Lillian Steinberg*
Astoria Workshop

Growing Older

People think of me as the Rock of Gibralter, large, solid, sturdy, and not one to worry about. I find as I age, although large and solid, pieces are chipped away. I'm not as sturdy, and hope someone is worrying about me.

A raging storm makes me think of the youth I struggled through. Then suddenly the sun peeks out from under a cloud, and in aging years I settled down to do the things I wanted to do. I therefore call these my sunshine years.

The calm sounds of the night remind me of the late years of my life. Both have the feeling of serenity, peace, and the knowledge of being.

Getting older has given me a self-assurance of my capabilities that I never had in youth.

When I am working with clay, it gives me a feeling of exaltation. In pounding, kneading and moulding, I'm creating something of earth to which I shall return.

—*Millie Goemann*

Growing Old

Growing old to me is a new experience like any other phase of life.
Growing old is like visiting a museum: one admires things of the past.
Being old is like an evening after a day of work.
It is like a beautiful sunset on a winter day or a vacation without responsibility, a time of leisure.
Being old is like fall time.
Being old is like taking inventory.
Being old is preparing for a long trip to the unknown.

—*Martha Rosenfelder*

Growing

Growing up is climbing up a ladder to an unknown peak. Growing old is like reaching the shore after a long and stormy voyage. You wonder what lies ahead and feel reluctant to leave the familiar ship.

Growing is a natural process of life. You are expanding
both in body and spirit. It is learning how to live,
and explore the unknown.
Experience is the greatest teacher. If you know that there
is no limit to acquiring knowledge, it can help you grow
young, not old.

—Norman Hofferman

9. *To imagine; to create "lies" that tell the truth; to play with words,
images, ideas, feelings, experiences; to fuse disparate fragments of experience into works that are harmonious, radiant, and whole; to integrate
intuition and knowledge, vision and observation, past and present,
imagination and reality:*

"I'm sitting quietly beneath a tall oak tree, listening to the
flapping and swooshing and gliding above my head, the rippling
plop-plopping and lapping close by, then suddenly there's a
crunching swirling beneath me, the patter of something approaching. I'm startled, I listen. Nothing. Just "shhh" whistling,
and I feel loose, I find myself diddling and daddling."

—Millie Goemann

Refuge

Early morning, I sit on my
    terrace upon the canal.
The sun is rising from the
    east, spreading its
irridescent rays upon the
    calm water.
A boat with its churning
    motor passes slowly by,
making the water swirl
    around. It kicks up the
frightened, fleeing fish.
They find a place of
    refuge, far from harm.
Why, then, can't I?

—Bea Lipsett

In the Garden

The assassin's knife
Plunges into its victim's back
Shedding blood on the roses

—*Julia Schubert*
Astoria Workshop

Mask

How I wish I could speak
And tell my master the things
He shouldn't do
And the things I wish he would do.

Couldn't he guide me gently
Instead of pulling forcefully on my leash?

When I bark and gaze at him—
If he only returned my gaze
He just might understand that I love and
    obey his every wish.
But he is not sensitive.
I am.

Still I keep on hoping that some day
I may penetrate his feelings, and that
He may in some small measure at least
Reciprocate the love and kindness
    I shower on him.

—*Aurelia Goldin*

Sounds Like My Life

"In 1938 I purchased a beautiful black print taffeta dress
that would rustle when I danced. We took the trolley car down-
town, the bells went clang, clang, clang as the trolley moved along.

"When the airplane was going down, the pain in my ears was such that I wanted to scream.

"When I was ten years old, twice, I rode in an ambulance to the hospital.

"Now the fire engine passes by at odd hours. Sometimes Lisa, my dog, yodels along with the siren. Napoleon, my other dog, growls if someone is on the other side of the door. I have had six dogs. Each one had his or her own personality. I have loved them all for their silly lovable ways. Each one becomes a part of your life at a different stage of your life: Tootsie, Fritzie, Skippy, Napoleon, and Lisa.

* * *

"I remember when I was six years old, in West Philadelphia, running after horse-drawn fire engines, and falling down into the sloshing water, getting it in my mouth.

"The milkman left the sled, minus the horse, across the street from our house. Everybody rode down the hill on the big sled, but everyone fell on top of me. At another time we played Red Light, a hide-and-go-seek game. I reached the gas lantern first, but someone ran after me and smashed my face into the lantern. Result—cracked front tooth.

"Rippling waves around the rowboat made the boat bounce up and down. The lightening flashed all around the house and the trees, making me nervous.

"Down in Florida when the sun sets, large bullfrogs come out and make a croaking sound."

—Frances Arluck, Astoria Workshop

10. *To reminisce, to review their lives:*
"I like the remembrance of family, and things that happened, and it comes back to you. I love that very much. Memories, and generation gaps, and family, and past and present and future we wrote about, and I love that."

—Irene Salamon

"There's such a—how shall I say?—misconception, and there's such a terribly youth-oriented society that so many people are so afraid: even saying the words 'senior citizens' frightens them, as if they don't want to get older. And sometimes I don't think they really know what it's all about because you can get older if you accept the fact that fortunately when you get older you can look back on things in the past and some of them relate to the present, which is very important and which most of us would not have thought about as much if we hadn't been in the workshop. But here we are made aware of the fact that you can get older and you can do things and you can live a life and be productive and be interesting and be with people."*

—Margaret Friedman

The tendency of the elderly toward self-reflection and reminiscence used to be thought of as indicating a loss of recent memory and therefore a sign of aging. However, in 1961 Robert Butler postulated that reminiscence in the aged was part of a normal life review process brought about by realization of approaching dissolution and death. It is characterized by the progressive return to consciousness of past experiences and particularly the resurgence of unresolved conflicts which can be looked at again and reintegrated. If the reintegration is successful, it can give new meaning to one's life and prepare one for death, by mitigating fear and anxiety ... In late life, people have a particularly vivid imagination and memory for the past and can recall with sudden and remarkable clarity early life events. There is a renewed ability to free-associate and bring up material from the unconscious. Individuals realize that their own personal myth of invulnerability and immortality can no longer be maintained. All of this results in a reassessment of life, which brings depression, acceptance, or satisfaction.

—Robert Butler & Myrna Lewis, *Aging and Mental Health*[6]

The memory that is not memory, but the application of a concordance to the Old Testament of the individual, (Proust) calls "voluntary memory." This is the uniform memory of the intelligence; and it can be reled on to reproduce for our gratified inspection those impressions of the past that were consciously and intelligently formed. It has no interest in the mysterious element of inattention that colors our most commonplace experiences. It presents the past in monochrome . . . *Involuntary memory* is explosive, "an immediate, total and delicious deflagration." It restores, not merely the past object, but the Lazarus that it charmed or tortured, not merely Lazarus and the object, but more because less, more because it abstracts the useful, the opportune, the accidental, because in its flame it has consumed Habit and all its works, and in its brightness revealed what the mock reality of experience can and never will reveal— the real. But involuntary memory is an unruly magician and will not be importuned. It chooses its own time and place for the performance of its miracle. I do not know how often this miracle recurs in Proust. I think twelve or thirteen times. But the first—the famous episode of the madeleine steeped in tea—would justify the assertion that his entire book is a monument to involuntary memory and the epic of its action. The whole of Proust's world comes out of a teacup. . . .

—Samuel Beckett, *Proust*[7]

The phenomenon of life review in old age appears simply as one form of consciousness—the autobiographical consciousness—which provides the old person with a retrospective version of the meaning of past events—a series of "metaphors of self" . . . The criterion of autobiographical truth is to be found not in science but in art. On these terms, the process of life review in old age ends in a fictionalized or mythic act of interpretation whereby it is possible to discover—better, create—an order of intelligibility in one's past, not by remembering it, but by interpreting it, indeed creating from it new forms of personal meaning.

—Harry Moody, *Reflections on the Living History Project*[5]

11. *To transmit their life experience to those who come after them, their children and grandchildren; to make socially important contributions of their knowledge of the past:*

"I believe that by recording our experiences, our grandchildren have a way of glancing at the past and they will probably derive a great deal of pleasure doing that. Also, they may realize that we are not more than just meeting for lunch, but getting together in an effort to share our experiences.

"We are not old, but simply citizens advanced in the many experiences of life—love, hate, death, life, happiness, all the things that comprise a long life."

—Margot Rodriguez

Writing an autobiography and making a spiritual will are practically the same thing.

—Sholem Aleichem, *The Great Fair*[8]

In their rememberings are their truths. The precise fact or the precise date is of small consequence. This is not a lawyer's brief nor an annotated sociological treatise. It is simply an attempt to get the story of the holocaust known as the Great Depression from an improvised battalion of survivors.

—Studs Terkel, *Hard Times*[9]

Oral history is a record of perceptions, rather than a re-creation of historical events. It can be employed as a factual source only if corroborated. The difficulty of cross-checking information does not detract, however, from its value for understanding perceptions and recovering levels of experience which are not normally available to historians. It offers almost the only feasible route for the retrieval of perceptions and experiences of whole groups of people who did not normally leave a written record. The major contribution of *Akenfield* and *Hard Times* is not their historical accuracy, but rather in their contribution to an understanding of human experience and social conditions.

—Tamara Haraven, The Search for Generational Memory: Tribal Rites in Industrial Society[10]

During the last two years of her life, my grandmother worked with me on an oral history of life and immigration to America "because I want my children and grandchildren should know a little more about the family before us. Zeydeh* used to like to talk about the past, he had a lot of

---

*Zeydeh: Yiddish for grandfather.

memories, but my children weren't too much interested to hear. But it was really interesting what Zeydeh had to say about his past, and little things that I remember from my old country, from my family life with my relatives, in my home. It really should be interesting to my children and my grandchildren where they come from, the roots. Sometimes Zeydeh would remember something, would say something in passing, but they didn't show interest that he should talk more about it. It didn't make him feel good about it because to him it meant something, and to me too. Why shouldn't my kids know where I come from and where Zeydeh comes from and how people lived in his time and the way we were raised and the customs there, and that we also had these things with us and practiced them as much as we could in our life together.

—Esther Schwartzman, Astoria Workshop

REFERENCES

1. Montale, E. The second life of art. *The New York Review of Books,* April 16, 1981.

2. Rilke, R. M. *The duino elegies.* Translated by J. B. Leishman and S. Spender. New York: Norton, 1963.

3. Wright, J. *The branch will not break.* Middletown, Conn.: Weslayan University Press, 1963.

4. Olsen, T. *Silences.* New York: Delacorte Press, 1978.

5. Moody, H. R. *Reflections on the Living History Project.* Unpublished paper, 1981.

6. Butler, R. & Lewis, M. *Aging and mental health.* St. Louis: C. V. Mosby, 1963.

7. Beckett, S. *Proust.* New York: Grove Press, 1931.

8. Aleichem, S. *The great fair.* Translated by T. Kahana. New York: Collier Books, 1970. First published in 1916.

9. Terkel, S. *Hard times.* New York: Avon Books, 1970.

10. Haraven, T. The search for generational memory: Tribal rites in industrial society. *Daedalus,* Fall 1978.

Chapter 6

MAGICAL PROPERTIES OF THE POEM

Rhythm and Sound

Paul Christensen

In Robert Duncan's book, *The Opening of the Field* (1984), there is this essential claim for the poem:

> First there is the power, and in the power
>   is the tone of tune,
> so that all of creation moves with
>   a music; the sound having its open
> door in the mind: but in the heart
>   lieth its fountain
> (as it doth also in Man).[1]

Since World War II, considerable attention has been paid to the nature of the poem, particularly that aspect of a poem which suggests it does more than communicate a conscious intention of a poet to a consciously alert reader. That something intangible and wordless transpires between the poem and the reader's deepest levels of being, levels far beyond articulable awareness of self which many would argue is the chief pleasure of the art, and perhaps the reason—regardless of the age or the hostility a society may express toward this art—the poem endures and accompanies each generation through its time on earth. It is in fact just this power of the poem to move a reader in ways that cannot be controlled or understood that explains the hostility a highly rational society expresses toward it; it is but one of many inexplicable forces that act upon the human being which cannot be ciphered and exploited. The poem remains one of those powerful amulets of the deep past whose charms upon the mind and heart are as potent today as they were when used by shamans of a distant epoch. It unnerves us to know that such a charm could survive the ages and come down to us with a new generation of fabricators anxious to make more of them. The poem is that nuisance mystery of language that arouses emotions the way nothing else can. In spite of all of society's efforts to do away with the poem—closing off the book publishers, shrinking back public money to subsidize small presses and regional writing, replacing liberal arts with vocationalism at all levels of education—the poem returns with the resilience and stubbornness of life itself. For centuries the poem has been driven out of the affairs of society, beginning with Europe's industrialism in the seventeenth century; since then, attacks upon this art have grown more shrill as society has tried to wean itself from nature and its old biological ties to the earth. When Whitman wrote his first preface to *Leaves of Grass* in 1855, he pleaded with his country to take a poet to its breast as passionately as the poet took the country to his own. The book was merely banned and the poet driven into a life of isolation among a few admirers and fanatic accolytes. His is the story of many of America's poets, perhaps the story of poetry throughout the West—unless that poet could prove himself loyal to authority and willing to write its official hymns of praise. If not, he was considered a double agent, an enemy in the camp of the righteous, using his old mantras and chants to spoil the discipline and rationality of the young, to turn his countrymen's hearts away from work toward love, foolishness, impracticality, toward rebellion, even revolution and the destruction of the state. All this is imputed to the poem and the poet who conceives: they are the mockers of rationalism when they are at their best.

But when we examine a poem to look for those latent powers to move the human being, one sees many interpenetrating aspects of the poem, none of which in isolation seems to reveal the root to the primordial. One looks at a poem's grammar and syntax and sees the evolution of language—a state of speech framed off in a political and cultural configuration. Spelling and puncutation are but fashions in language. Use of titles, typographical flourishes, and conventions are the mutable characteristics of print technology and educational norms. Semantic statement is a critical stance in a moment of social time. Once these levels of the poem have been peeled back, stripped from the core of the poem, there remain two elements that are not so easily tagged and sorted—the rhythms of the poem, and the sounds of the text, the isolated phonemes, the multilayered affects of their aggregates in dipthongs, syllables, words, phrases, sentences, stanzas, and the total poem.

As for the rhythm, there is a long critical tradition that has produced a noble body of literature on the use of stresses in a poem, known as prosody. And from it we can learn much about the meaning and effect of rhythm. "The view I take," Harvey Gross wrote in *Sound and Form in Modern Poetry,*

> is that meter, and prosody in general, is itself meaning. Rhythm is neither outside of a poem's meaning nor an ornament to it. Rhythmic structures are expressive forms, cognitive elements, communicating those experiences which the rythmic consciousness can alone communicate: empathic human responses to time in its passage.[2]

This position nicely restates Emerson's own memorable description:

> . . . it is not metres, but a metre-making argument that makes a poem—a thought so passionate and alive that like the spirit of a plant or an animal it has an architecture of its own, and adorns nature with a new thing. The thought and the form are equal in the order of time, but in the order of genesis the thought is prior to the form.[3]

Rhythm in the poem is an emotional response to thinking— and it will rush or slow according to the poet who experiences his thinking as he writes. There is a natural and organic relation between the thought of the language and the effect it has upon the poet, and if the poet is alive to his thought—to be a poet assures us that he is—the reader will feel the same response as well, and find his response reproduced in the pace of the language that unfolds the argument. So the rhythm of the poem is a twofold communication—it responds to something thought and felt, and directs the response of a reader. It is the record of the pulse of the writer, and a reinforcement of the emotional response of the reader. Disembodied from the poem, rhythm is a succession of stresses and rests—a subtle oscillation that when traced far enough back to a source ends in the heart that varies its beats to changes within the human organism. The shifting rate of the heart is encoded into the language of an emotional experience; if correct in all particulars, the rates of stress and their frequency in language will capture the universal response to an experience. The poet will have found the right human reaction to a thought, discovered through his metrical experiments and formulations of how the heart responds, anyone's heart, to the precise intellectual events transpiring in the mind on a particular occasion. This remarkable generality of the poem—that it can discern universal responses to emotional events—is one of the indestructible values of the poem.

To put it one final way, the rhythms within a poem constitute a graph of the respiration and metabolic consequences that an experience forces upon the human organism. It is the inked out equivalents of the peaks and scratchy profiles of the lie detector test—which also measures pulse and blood pressure shifts as a mind takes in and gives back response to stressful and emotionally charged experiences. Disembodied from their matter, they are nothing more than empty ciphers and calculations resting on nothing. They require the substance of words and meanings of words in order to have a life; because they are themselves a code of how the animal organism of a human, its body and blood, its nerves and muscles, have drawn up and tensed and squirmed under the impact of jeopardizing or arousing changes within its mental makeup.

In the rhythmic record of a good poem is the ideal response

to emotion; if the reader is in any way cut off from that emotion, unable for any reason to respond with the same vigor and candor to the experience, the poem offers a guide to the reader how to respond; tells him what the species itself would do under ideal circumstances—that is, in circumstances unblemished by repression, phobia, psychosis, trauma, extraneous stress or pressure—with the sudden confrontation of this novelty or crisis in the perceptual focus of the mind. The poet who captures that true and universal response offers an idealized emotional response, one that most clearly and most energetically incorporates the crisis or pleasure into its makeup, is moved the most freely and healthfully to an imbalance or sudden unexpected gift of feeling, and the reader, whose apparatus has been damaged or transformed, will hear, distantly or through many filters, the perfect response he is incapable of, but knows all the same to be the truth. In rhythm is kept the secret of our emotions, which the poet glimpses when he correctly orders the stresses and rests of his language.

A child who has not known the experience captured within the poem cannot repeat its response through a correct reading of its rhythmic structure, its subtext of emotional stresses and rests. Nor can the adult whose powers of response have been blunted by illness or psychological deformity. To read a poem effectively is a test of the powers of feeling in a reader, of one's state of readiness and generosity, one's sensuous tuning. The silent reader misses the impact of the rhythmic encoding of the poem, and thereby puts at a distance his powers of response. Our present fashion of reading silently, of learning to keep the lips and tongue from moving, of remaining impassive in a chair, limp and stock-still, is a culturally conditioned numbness trained into us in school, as a way of blunting the awful powers of the poem from reaching us. We have been told the proper reading of a text is to be frozen to its charms, to pretend to feel nothing, only to look for putative argument, the poem's linguistic forensics and attitudinal flourishes, instead of its grunts and animal squirms, which when reproduced in us through passionate reading aloud, the body fully in the act of the reading, with arms and legs moving sinuously and in rhythmic trance to the poem, stir us to depths we do not otherwise know. But in blunting the poem we have blunted life, and delivered ourselves up numb to a social order that requires our mute affiliation.

There remains in our poem the aspect of its sounds, the bits and particles of voice arrayed in endless combinations to make up the total sound of the poem. And of its sound and sonic embellishments much has been written, but in a scattered and piecemeal fashion. There are very few critical texts that have plumbed the nature of sound in human speech or in the musically enriched speech of the poem. We know that certain formulations of sound in speech have magical powers. The powers of oratory have fascinated critics from classical Athens to our own day—the sibilance, alliteration, repetition, incantatory monotony of a powerful speaker seem to lower the audience's psyche into a dark recess of enchantment and submission, while the speaker performs all sorts of tricks upon consciousness and forms opinions and directs emotion, demands homage and obedience as the audience sleeps contentedly under the hypnotic spell of the sounds emanating from the speaker's engulfing voice. Demosthenes was a spell-worker and could reduce an audience to any level of childlike submission he wished; Hitler's delirious speeches were as good as liquor on the brains of his listeners—they fawned and moaned over his words, over his orphic song of hatred and revenge, and were reduced to whimpers and helpless shouting long before he had finished with them.

But for more exacting analysis and revelation as to the meaning of sound in the poem, one must go to the arcana of the poets—in whose flashes and brief asides are telling summations of the power of sound. Perhaps even Plato enters here: he burned his manuscripts in disgust that the poem rivaled nature in making copies of ideal forms, only to distort, and to mislead the people by inept imitation. Perhaps he too disguised his real purpose; the powers of poetry were known to him, and it was a rational utopia he intended to fashion out of Athenian Greece, the strict conduct of which could only be subverted by the feral enchantments of the poem. It was burned not out of despair at its poor reproduction of natural forms, but rather, because it was as much an impediment to merely rational order then as it is now. He is the first to censor poetry in our record of Western life—the pyre has been fueled ever since. But it is at the first thrust of industrialization in England that we begin to see a guardianship of the poem arise, among Romantic poets disenchanted with the newly regimented order of their society. Blake's *Marriage of Heaven and Hell* is a combination of the powers of intellect (heaven) with the enchantments of the body (hell), among which are the brute sounds of the human voice and throat. In the opening song of *Songs of Experience*, he declaims, "Behold the voice of the bard, who present, past, and future sees." The voice was in possession of all time, we should note, and sounded the flute notes of immutable human existence. Shelley's *Defence of Poetry* observes that the sound of poetry is a direct transcription of the process of imagination, which borrowing from Coleridge, is nothing less than the esemplastic powers of the universe, the energy of synthesis in which all life participates. The Imagination, "the infinite I AM," to quote Coleridge, is deposited in the human brain, a mere smear of the substance, which in other parts of the universe seethes in quantity and brings forth galaxies and miraculous phenomena. Sounding the imagination therefore plumbs life's source, the life serum which brings about creation, manifests the invisible into palpable matter, turns intangible vision to substance. Its nature is one of paradoxes; it is the voice made of air, pushing air through two reedlike parallel structures of the throat called the glottis, tuning pitch by means of air pressure. Sound is only vibrations of invisible gas, undetected by any other sense but the one tucked beside the brain, the ear, whose tiny stirrup and anvil rattle exactly to the wave vibrations that come to it, transferring these vibrations along nerve channels to the brain for sorting and assimilation: an evanescent thing made and delivered on the air, but palpable once inside the head and coursing through the brain.

Sound stripped of all meaning still possesses meaning. The ancient religions are eloquent on the function of the vowels—the universe is said to vibrate in one sacred key—perhaps middle C, which when reproduced by the human voice unlocks the passages between an individual and the great beyond. Hence the purgative and resuscitating powers of chanting a mantra, droned in the key of the universe as the means for letting one's self flow out into the fields of the Not-I. The whirling dancers of the Sufi religion believe there is a sound that opens a particular sense; they chant a sensory alphabet which unstoppers the body's inlets to admit prana energy to revitalize the spirit and flesh.

All the world's religions use sound to heal and renew, by dissolving the alert consciousness, by blunting its tentacles of sensory attention. Sound, by repetition and by sustained expression, instantly reduces the focal range of consciousness, as a fine membraneous layer of passive awareness arises and replaces it. Behind it are the great banks of memory and latent, mute intelligence that are brought forward into the unfocused half-light of mind. Sound, when applied by a trained healer, can put the mind to rest in a far and remote state of cognition where all articulation and categorized reality cease, and a primal state of animal passivity rises up. In this state a nearly perfect sensuality is felt, the powers of feeling are given complete expression, and all means of governance and willful inhibition are erased. Hence, the speaking in tongues, barking, rolling in ecstasy, and other deep-state manifestations of fundamentalist religion in rural America, and in many religions of Africa and Asia.

Sound is dangerous as well. Sound control is a necessity of industrial life in the West, not because it damages the ear, but because it lulls the worker into that same animal state, as he is saturated with the murmurs of machines and metal equipment. He slips beneath the disk of consciousness into the primal seas of his animal nature, as a machine clips off a finger or a hand or a leg or sends millions of dollars of equipment to their ruin. In place of that deadly, luring murmur, that orphic whisper out of the dynamos of the factory, there comes the insistent, cheerful tinkle of Muzak with its calculated rhythmic acceleration in 15-minute intervals, to ward off the dark satanic drone of nature.

When Faulkner was very young, writing his first novel, he was a night watchman at a construction site, where he stole a few hours to write as he leaned against an electric generator. This lethal hum brought forth his powers of ecstatic lyrical prose, a concentration on his own dream content. Delivered from that sort of hardship by the success of his book, he wrote another in silence, sweating over his desk in an empty room, unaware that he missed his greatest muse—the dynamo. Years later, he told an interviewer he almost wished he had purchased a generator and kept it droning beside him as he wrote.

In one of our greatest visionary poems of the Industrial Age, Whitman's *Song of Myself*, the visionary journey is begun with this invocation:

I believe in you my soul, the other I am must not abase itself to you,
And you must not be abased to the other.

Loafe with me on the grass, loose the stop from your throat,
Not words, not music or rhyme I want, not custom or lecture, not
   even the best,
Only the lull I like, the hum of your valved voice.[4]

And with that lull, there ensues a lowering down into animal consciousness wherein many seamless connections are felt and seen between the human being and his long evolutionary past, the animal continuum, the mineral and vegetable trailings in the formation of his species, to the distant star stuff of which he is made, as he goes out further and further into Coleridge's infinite I am to discover on his own, in American surroundings, the same truth—a truth shared by mystics, shamans, healers, witch doctors, Sufi dancers, primordial man, contemporary Western man. The hadic doors are opened by the sound of a human voice, the sesame of vowels uttered resonantly as the consciousness, that newly acquired organ of evolution, fades out and the rest of nature looms forward to release its infinite content into the small grasp of human perception.

I am the poet of the Body [Whitman wrote in *Song of Myself*], and
   I am the poet of the Soul,
The pleasures of heaven are with me and the pains of hell are with
   me,
The first I graft and increase upon myself, the latter I translate
   into a new tongue.

Later in the poem, having already reached visionary apex and descending once more he writes,

> A call in the midst of the crowd,
> My own voice, orotund sweeping and final.
> Come my children,
> Come my boys and girls, my women, household and
>   intimates,
> Now the performer launches his nerve, he has pass'd his
>   prelude on the reed within.
> Easily written loose-fingered chords—I feel the thrum
>   of your climax and close.
> My head slues round on my neck,
> Music rolls, but not from the organ,
> Folks are around me, but they are no household of
>   mine.[5]

In a brief but influential 1950 essay, *Projective Verse*, Charles Olson remarked that the poet possesses a memory in the ear; and suggests that he first composes by sound. That is, he is led forward by the patterning of sounds remembered by the ear that originally heard them in nature, which are crafted in sequence at the heat of composition. Only by grudging compromise is anything like a semantic scheme accorded to these sonic particles. Olson seems to be suggesting that the poet sings a primordial song out of his gathered sounds, and sense enters as a secondary intention of this initial mosaic of sounds. The poet Robert Duncan, following Olson's lead, wrote a poem entitled *An Owl is an Only Bird of Poetry,* in which he remarked:

Figure 1
The vowels are physical
corridors of the imagination
emitting passionately
breaths of flame. In a poem
the vowels appear like
the flutterings of an owl
caught in a web and give
aweful intimations of
eternal life.

Figure 2
The consonants are a church of
hands interlocking, stops
and measures of fingerings
that confine the spirit to
articulations of space and time.[6]

The vowels are the very keys the Sufis use to cleanse the portals of the body; the vowels lulled Whitman to vision; the vowels here in Duncan's poem are the "physical corridors" out of individual life into eternal life. They illuminate the role of Orpheus, who voiced these eternal sounds and escaped Hades once more to the light. The vowels are corridors into the deep primordial sources of human identity, made culturally finite and localized by the arrangement of consonants around them. But their plumbings, their sonorous clangor in the poem tugs at the alert and defensive psyche of the listener/reader and begins to draw him down into the great subhuman depths of nature, where the energy of one is the energy of all.

Semantic speech is, if you will, a faint disguise over the elemental sound keys of all of life, the animal continuum preserved in the five cosmic links of our speech, which the poem constantly teases into active focus by sibilance, repetition, alliteration, consonantal and dissonantal elaboration, sifting the gritty pointed controls of elemental sound through consonants, as if one rolled a pan of muddy water in which a few nuggets of gold were present. In the vowels and their endless, inexhaustible permutations through consonantal context, the human descends into the animal universe once again, reverses his evolution, is bathed in he waters of universal life and unsorted visionary experience.

One could question all these parameters of the poem, in the spirit of contemporary skepticism, but one could not remove this condition of our lives—that in embryonic formation our only true sense—the only one not blocked by conditions of the womb, is of hearing—and we hear those fuzzy, water-logged syllables of our mother's speech before we know the meaning or substance of her communication. But we hear the murmurs of the universe, our amniotic sea's own voice, pumped through the girderings and thick muscular walls surrounding us, the voice of the mother, primordial, distant as thunder, profound, earth-shattering, and sweeter than any other sense in our memory. It is even there that the poem plumbs for vision and seductive lures, reducing us to baby lengths of consciousness again, but to so much more, as well; as confirmed by the long history of mysticism and incantation, of magic, spells, witchcraft, and all the sister arts of poetry.

We must put back the layers of the poem, reintegrate it on the page, fold the book shut, resume our normal, controlled state of consciousness, and conclude in summation that it is no wonder the poem is the object of our contumely, despised, rejected, run out of the classroom, out of the cities, out of memory by whatever lies ready to hand in the defense of modern, industrial society. But it is a weed growing out of the mute earth, and cannot be destroyed. It is denied because it is among the most potent forces in our lives, and can undo all the work of our sciences and arts and civilizations in one sound of its voice, refreshing our vital innards, arousing our old defiant energies, putting us once more in touch with our primal lives and our animal senses.

But a nation guarding its treasure and surpluses of food and luxury against a starving world cannot sleep, either. Therefore, there is militant avoidance of sleep and dream, of the depths of poetry, the depths of renewal and replenishment of energies. The geopolitical instability in which America broods sphinxlike at its own door, armed, cautious, defensive, is reflected in the starved, sleepless, dreamless hollows of the individual citizen's life. Poetry brings round only the most broken; it is a last medicine to the troubled and disheartened, when it could be the elixir of healthy, balanced people in a healthy balanced nation only casually armed against lawless neighbors, not armed against an angry, grieving, and starving world.

The lover of poetry, properly speaking, is a wild organism in love with primitive energy and deep states of irrational experience. But he is also dressed, in possession of feeling and response, and capable of all the work assigned to the contemporary working citizen. To deny poetry is to deny access to the mystery of one's life. The patient who comes to a poetry therapist and weeps uncontrollably over the poem and cannot even interpret its semantic garnishments, has read it correctly and profoundly all the same—has heard nature mutter in some few of its vowels and roll through its rhythmic formulations, and has found himself, however disconnected or broken, made whole in one brief ecstatic, tearful moment. Let that explain over and over again why the poem is at once beautiful and grotesque, adored and hated, embraced and denied. The more we try to escape from nature, the more the poem chases after us with its leaves and vines, its old bleatings and grunts, its starry stuff stucco'd over its vowels and potent enchantments. To return once more to Whitman:

> Have you reckon'd a thousand acres much? have you reckon'd the earth much?
> Have you practis'd so long to learn to read?
> Have you felt so proud to get at the meaning of poems?
> Stop this day and night with me and you shall possess the origin of all poems,
> You shall possess the good of the earth and sun (there are millions of suns left)
> You shall no longer take things at second or third hand, nor look through the eyes of the dead, nor feed on the spectres of books,
> You shall not look through my eyes either, nor take things from me,
> You shall listen to all sides and filter them from your self.[7]

REFERENCES

1. Duncan, R. Ground work: Before the war. In *The opening of the field.* New York: New Directions, 1984.

2. Gross, H. *Sound and form in modern poetry.* Ann Arbor: University of Michigan Press, 1964.

3. Emerson, R. W. The poet. In *Essays, second series.* Boston: Ticknor and Fields, 1868.

4. Whitman, W. Song of myself. In *Leaves of grass.* Mount Vernon, New York: Peter Pauper Press, 1891.

5. *Ibid.*

6. Duncan, R. An owl is an only bird of poetry. In *Bending the bow.* New York: New Directions, 1968.

7. Whitman, op.cit.

Chapter 7

THE USE OF THE PSALMS IN PSYCHOTHERAPY

Sheila Fling

The Psalms of the Bible provide a wealth of poetry that seems conducive to mental and physical health and healing. I first learned of the healing potential of the Psalms from their skillful application by my father in his own life and in his pastoral counseling. For years they have fostered my own wellness, and more recently I have begun to use them in my private practice of clinical psychology. Here I first want to consider some assumptions and precautions in their use, secondly to suggest some current psychotherapeutic techniques with which they can be integrated, and finally to present some specific examples for a variety of disorders and problems-in-living.

ASSUMPTIONS AND PRECAUTIONS

Some people might question the use of scripture in scientific disciplines such as psychology and medicine. It is, however, consistent with the assumptions of transpersonal psychology (Tart, 1975; Walsh & Vaughan, 1980), the "fourth force" in psychology, which has developed chronologically after the psychoanalytic, learning, and humanistic/existential theories. Abraham Maslow (1970), Carl Jung (1933), Victor Frankl (1957), Roberto Assagioli (1971), and other transpersonal psychologists have maintained that we have not dealt with the whole person until we have dealt with the transcendent or spiritual dimension of the psyche, and that this is indeed the ultimate resource in the healing and actualization of the person.

Certainly we must heed the precaution of Victor Frankl, however, that we not impose transpersonal assumptions nor any particular spiritual outlook on our clients. We must respect the right of each to form their own beliefs and make their own choices. The rich poetry of the Psalms can be healing, however, particularly for those already following the Jewish or Christian paths.

This literature can also be meaningful to those subscribing to the Oriental religions or to the philosophical view of mysticism in general, that is, the assumption of a transcendent and yet immanent Oneness beyond and within the apparent dualities and multiplicities of our everyday existence. On the surface, such an abstract concept might seem contradicted by the Psalms' portrayal of a personal God, who might be rejected by some clients and therapists as limiting the concept of the transcendent, anthropomorphizing God, and making the Infinite separate and external to oneself. I submit instead that the abstract and personal concepts of God are compatible, that both can promote health, and that we can use one or the other or, ideally, both, in therapy, depending on the client's openness to this paradoxical position.

For example, Sufism (Kahn, 1981), Bhakti Hinduism (Anderson, 1960), Pure Land Buddhism (Anderson, 1960), and the mystical branches of Judaism (Eisenberg, 1973) and Christianity (Tillich, 1957) conceive the Ultimate as transcending and not limited to but yet including the aspect of personhood. Such a view allows the healing advantages of both the I-Thou relationship (Buber, 1958) and the realization of oneness with the Infinite. Bringing this interpretation to the Psalms thus can allow for their use for those of the Oriental religions or mystical philosophy as well as expanding their meaning for those of the Judeo-Christian tradition.

In addition to respecting the client's beliefs and adapting

the personal and/or abstract concepts of God to those beliefs, another precaution is handling therapeutically the many images of punishment and war that appear in the Psalms. Psychological research has shown the baneful effects of punishment (Parke, 1977) which can be translated as punishment from the feared vengeance of a wrathful God to a concept like the Hindu idea of "karma" or the natural, holistic, and systemic "boomerang" consequences of fragmentation and alienation from the Whole. As for references to warfare, I would agree with Carl Jung that our only "enemies" are the unintegrated and projected "shadow" aspects of ourselves. It seems crucial, perhaps today especially, to remember with the Sufis that the only "holy war" is the symbolic one within ourselves when we are not "at one" with the Infinite One. Used in this way, the images of punishment and war in the Psalms can lead to wholeness and health.

INTEGRATION WITH THERAPY TECHNIQUES

Bearing in mind these assumptions and precautions, I want now to suggest some practical ideas for using the Psalms and integrating them with contemporary psychotherapeutic techniques to promote health and healing. Individual tailoring to fit the client's needs and aesthetic values is, of course, most important. Clients can search for Psalms that have the most meaning for them, or choose from those suggested by the therapist. They can select from the many translations available and combine, alter, or even paraphrase for maximum personal cogency. Proper nouns of more familiar rivers, mountains, and cities can be substituted for those in the Psalms. Clients can free-associate to the Psalm, fantasize, and develop the poetic images in terms of their life specifics. Music background and art stimuli can be helpful for some.

Meditation is perhaps the most obvious technique (Carrington, 1977) for use with the Psalms. Writing the Psalm on a card and memorizing it allows for brief meditations interspersed throughout the day (at a traffic light or in a crisis situation, for example) as well as for regular, formal, daily periods of contemplation. Brief phrases or a single word from the passage can also be used in the "concentrative" type of meditation (Naranjo & Ornstein, 1971). For example, Psalm 131:2 can be helpful for anxiety, depression, insomnia, substance abuse, and compulsive eating: "I am content and at peace. As a child lies quietly in its mother's arms, so my heart is quiet within me" (Good News Bible, 1976, p. 685). Linking the mentally repeated phrases with the quiet, ever-present rhythm of the breathing can be especially effective. "(Inhaling) I am content (exhaling) and at peace. (Inhaling) As a child lies quietly in its mother's arms, (exhaling) so my heart is quiet within me."

Hypnosis and self-hypnosis provide an alternative technique for therapeutic use of the Psalms. Because of autonomy and dependency issues, however, except in emergencies I prefer to use hypnosis only to teach self-hypnosis, and I recommend the naturalistic, permissive, or Ericksonian (Zeig, 1985) approach.

When meditation and hypnosis have negative connotations for the client or therapist, one can substitute systematic muscle relaxation training (Jacobson, 1974) combined with affirmations and/or with guided or spontaneous visual, auditory, tactile, and kinesthetic imagery (Shorr, 1974) evoked by the Psalm.

Gendlin's (1978) focusing technique can also be used with the Psalms. In a deeply relaxed state, one focuses in a global way on a whole problem area without analysis or judgment. When the mind wanders to specifics, it is gently brought back to the overall dwelling upon "all that about so-and-so" until an insight comes to solve the problem or present it in a new way. A line from Psalm 81:7, "From my hiding place in the storm, I answered you" (Good News Bible, 1976, p. 649), led me to suggest "From your hiding place in this storm, answer me" for the focusing technique. If one believes and persists, an answer comes—a solution or at least a new perspective or meaning out of the chaos.

Gestalt therapy techniques (Perls, 1973) are also applicable to the Psalms: exaggeration, repetition, "becoming" the image, dancing the meaning, etc. I almost always recommend that first person singular pronouns and present tense verbs be used in the Psalm to increase the sense of personal applicability and awareness of feelings in the here and now.

The Psalms also lend themselves readily to cognitive restructuring (Maultsby & Ellis, 1974) i.e., catching one's "stinking thinking" and substituting an affirmation to change one's perspective and hence, the emotions.

EXAMPLES OF APPLICATIONS

With this variety of techniques to use in therapeutic application of the Psalms, consider now some examples for specific disorders. A physician referred to me, for stress-management training, a sixty-year-old woman with several physical disorders and many more imaginary ones. She was one of the most anxious people I've seen, and broke into tears in every session. For 6 weeks we established rapport and explored her circumstances and feelings while she began fast-walking and practicing systematic relaxation, self-hypnosis, cognitive restructuring, and meditation using the breath and the word "calm" for the mental focus.

She improved markedly, but a new series of stressors appeared in her life: her husband's serious illness, her only daughter's first pregnancy late in life accompanied by a move to a new house and financial problems, all in the midst of Christmas holidays! She struggled to maintain her new practices, but some of the anxiety and tearfulness returned. She mentioned having been to church over the holidays, and after exploring her beliefs I suggested five Psalms for her to consider integrating with her disciplines. Psalm 27 struck the strongest cord. I had suggested the poetic Revised Standard Version:

> The Lord is my light and my salvation; whom shall I fear?
> The Lord is the refuge of my life; of whom shall I be afraid?
> . . . Though a host encamp against me, my heart shall not
> fear; Though war arise against me, yet will I be confident.
> One thing have I asked of the Lord, that will I seek after;
> that I may dwell in the house of the Lord all the days of
> my life, to behold the beauty of the Lord, and to inquire in
> his temple. For he will hide me in his shelter in the day of
> trouble; he will conceal me under the cover of his tent, he
> will set me high upon a rock. And now my head shall be
> lifted up above my enemies around about me [or within
> me]; And I will offer in his tent sacrifices with shouts of

joy; I will sing and make melody to the Lord (*The Holy Bible*, 1962, p. 674).

The client returned with a modern paraphrase she found in Brandt and Kent's (1973) *Psalms Now:*

> With the living and eternal God as my goal and guide fear and anxiety preempt no place in my life. All the evil in the world is not able to destroy Him, nor can it destroy anyone within His loving embrace. The very legions of hell lay siege to my soul, only to be thwarted by a power far greater. I have one primary and ultimate desire: to abide within the love and acceptance of God. Within His tender care I know I am safe. Thus I shall stand tall regardless of threatening enemies and the tyranny of evil. I will counter the subtle voices of temptation with exclamations of praise to my God (p. 43).

She had incorporated this into her meditation and self-hypnosis, and the last sentence added new meaning to her cognitive restructuring as she "countered the subtle voices" of her negative thoughts by using them as cues to alert her to substitute "exclamations of praise."

> The paraphrase of Psalm 61 that she liked included this: I cannot find peace or security until I lose myself in something or someone that is greater than I. Draw me more deeply into Your life and purpose; only then will I find shelter from the tempests of this fearful and uncertain existence (Brandt & Kent, 1973, p. 99).

She then began some activities outside her own home and family to "lose herself in something greater," and after a few more weeks of practicing her now more meaningful habits, we terminated therapy. Follow-up contacts at 1 and 6 months indicated continued improvement with the added benefits of weight loss, a new hairstyle, and much more youthful, serene, and healthy appearance. Her referring physician wrote of her "significant improvement."

Another older woman who lived alone in the country was phobic of being bitten by a snake or spraining her ankle on the rocks and not being able to get to the phone for help. She found Psalm 91:9–13 perfect for her situation but substituted first person singular pronouns:

> You have made the Lord your defender, the Most High your habitation, and so no disaster will strike you, no violence will come near your home. God will put his angels in charge of you to protect you wherever you go. They will hold you up with their hands to keep you from hurting your feet on the stones. You will trample down lions and snakes, fierce lions and poisonous snakes (*Good News Bible*, 1976, p. 656).

At the same time she heeded the story of Satan's tempting Jesus to foolishly test this Psalm by throwing Himself off the pinnacle of the temple (Matthew 4:1–7). She took the practical precautions of buying boots to prevent turning her ankle, learning to identify poisonous snakes, and posting emergency directions to her home on her phone!

Other beautiful Psalms abound for dealing with anxiety, stress, and phobias, but turn now to some examples for guilt, grief, and depression.

Psalm 103:10–13 reminds us,

> He does not punish us as we deserve or repay us according to our sins and wrongs. As high as the sky is above the earth, so great is his love for those who have reverence for him. As far as the east is from the west, so far does he remove our sins from us. As a father is kind to his children, so the Lord is kind to those who honor him (*Good News Bible*, 1976, pp. 662–663).

How excellent these phrases are for meditation and for cognitive restructuring when torturing oneself with guilt: "As high as the sky is above the earth . . . as far as the east is from the west . . . as a father is kind to his children." Psalm 40:1–3 has similar potent phrases and images for countering depression especially when present tense verbs are substituted:

> I waited patiently for the Lord: he inclined to me and heard my cry. He drew me up from the desolate pit, out of the miry bog, and set my feet upon a rock, making my steps secure. He put a new song in my mouth, a song of praise to our God (*The Holy Bible*, 1962, p. 686).

For coping with grief, Psalm 43:3, 6–8, 11 allows opportunity for Gestalt techniques of repetition, exaggeration, and catharsis, and then moves on to affirmation.

> Day and night I cry, and tears are my only food; . . . my heart is breaking and so I turn my thoughts to him. He has sent waves of sorrow over my soul; chaos roars at me like a flood, like waterfalls thundering down to the Jordan from Mount Hermon and Mount Mizar. May the Lord show his constant love during the day, so that I may have a song at night, a prayer to the God of my life. . . . Why am I so sad? Why am I so troubled? I will put my hope in God, and once again I will praise him, my savior and my God (*Good News Bible*, 1976, p. 621).

Other phrases can be helpful with substance abuse and compulsive eating: "He satisfieth the longing soul, and filleth the hungry soul with goodness" (*The Holy Bible*, Psalm 107:9, p. 712). "My whole being desires you; like a dry, worn-out, and waterless land, my soul is thirsty for you. . . . My soul will feast and be satisfied" (*Good News Bible*, 1976, Psalm 63:1 & 5, pp. 633–634). "Open your mouth wide, and I will fill it. . . . I would feed you with the finest of the wheat, and with honey from the rock I would satisfy you (*The Holy Bible*, 1962, Psalm 81:10 & 16, pp. 719–720). For stopping other unwanted habits and thoughts, Psalm 58:6–7 has vivid imagery: "Break the teeth of these fierce lions, O God. May they disappear like water draining away; may they be crushed like weeds on a path" (*Good News Bible*, 1976, p. 631).

For dealing with discouragement in difficult tasks and seemingly insurmountable obstacles, the following poetic phrases from the *Good News Bible* (1976) can be used with self-hypnosis or cognitive restructuring techniques, and the dual phrases link easily with a breathing meditation. "Those who wept as they went out carrying the seed will come back singing for joy, as they bring in the harvest" (Psalm 126:6, p. 683). "The hills melt like wax before the Lord" (Psalm 97:5, p. 659). "He breaks down doors of bronze and smashes iron bars" (Psalm 107:16, p. 668). "[He] changes rocks into pools of water and solid cliffs into flowing streams" (Psalm 114:8, p. 673). "He divided the sea and took them through it; He made the waters stand like walls" (Psalm 78:13, p. 645). (Substituting present tense verbs and first person singular pronouns in this and the next example seems most effective).

Psalm 121:3–7 is perfect for hypnosis or self-hypnosis for insomnia:

> Your protector is always awake. The protector of Israel never dozes or sleeps. The Lord will guard you; he is by your side to protect you. The sun will not hurt you during the day, nor the moon during the night. The Lord will protect you from all danger; he will keep you safe (*Good News Bible*, 1976, p. 682).

Psalm 57:8 is useful for excessive sleeping or for apathy: "Wake up my soul! Wake up, my harp and lyre! I will wake up the sun" (*Good News Bible*, 1976, p. 631).

For preventing and healing physical illness, Psalms 103 and 91 are magnificent poems. Psalm 102:3–7, 11–12, & 27 allows catharsis and grief in serious illness and then resolves in a ringing affirmation:

> My life is disappearing like smoke; my body is burning like fire. I am beaten down like dry grass; I have lost my desire for food. I groan aloud; I am nothing but skin and bones. I am like a wild bird in the desert, like an owl in abandoned ruins. I lie awake; I am like a lonely bird on a housetop. . . . My life is like the evening shadows; I am like dry grass. But

you, O Lord are king forever; . . . you are always the same, and your life never ends (*Good News Bible*, 1976, pp. 661–662).

For dealing with aging, one can use Psalm 92:12–14 or this passage from Psalm 73:25–26, "What else do I have in heaven but you? Since I have you, what else could I want on earth? My mind and body may grow weak, but God is my strength; he is all I ever need" (*Good News Bible*, 1976, p. 642). For coping with death, Psalm 103:14–17 says,

> He knows what we are made of; he remembers that we are dust. As for us, our life is like grass. We grow and flourish like a wild flower; then the wind blows on it, and it is gone—no one sees it again. But for those who honor the Lord, his love lasts forever (*Good News Bible*, 1976, p. 663).

Victor Frankl (1963) described the dignity and serenity of some of his Nazi-prison campmates as they walked into the gas chambers reciting Psalm 23, "Yea, though I walk through the valley of the shadow of death, I will fear no evil: for thou art with me" (*The Holy Bible*, p. 663). Psalms 17:15 and 139:18 can help in facing death joyfully (or for insomnia): "I shall behold thy face in righteousness; when I awake, I shall be satisfied with beholding thy form" (*The Holy Bible*, p. 666). "When I awake, I am still with you" (*Good News Bible*, 1976, p. 689).

Finally, for dealing with two crucial fears for all of us on planet Earth today, read Psalm 102:25–27 in relation to ecological ruin and the following passages (Psalm 46 and 98:8–9) from the *Good News Bible* (1976) in light of the possibility of nuclear devastation. (The city or house of God can be interpreted as the individual in whom the Infinite dwells.)

> God is our shelter and strength, always ready to help in times of trouble. So we will not be afraid, even if the earth is shaken and mountains fall into the ocean depths; even if the seas roar and rage, and the hills are shaken by the violence. There is a river that brings joy to the city of God, to the sacred house of the Most High. God is in that city, and

it will never be destroyed; at early dawn he will come to its aid. Nations are terrified, kingdoms are shaken; God thunders and the earth dissolves. The Lord Almighty is with us; the God of Jacob is our refuge. Come and see what the Lord has done. See what amazing things he has done on earth. He stops wars all over the world; he breaks bows, destroys spears, and sets shields on fire. "Stop fighting [or be still]," he says, "and know that I am God, supreme over the nations, supreme over the world" (pp. 623–624). Roar, sea, and every creature in you; sing, earth, and all who live on you! Clap your hands, you rivers; you hills, sing together with joy before the Lord, because he comes to rule the earth. He will rule the peoples of the world with justice and fairness (p. 660).

In summary, using the assumptions of transpersonal psychology and the precautions discussed in this paper, especially with regard to respecting the client's beliefs, the rich poetry of the Psalms can be integrated with a number of current psychotherapeutic techniques to foster mental and physical health and healing. The potential of this form of poetry therapy seems indeed worthy of further application and development.

REFERENCES

Anderson, J. N. D., (Ed.). *The world's religions.* Grand Rapids: Wm. B. Eerdmans, 1960.

Assagioli, R. *Psychosynthesis.* New York: Viking, 1971.

Brandt, L., & Kent, C. *Psalms now.* St. Louis: Concordia, 1973.

Buber, M. *I and thou.* New York: Charles Scribner's, 1958.

Carrington, P. *Freedom in meditation.* Garden City, NY: Anchor Press, 1977.

Eisenberg, D. *Judaism: A mystic approach.* Boston: Little, Brown, & Co., 1973.

Frankl, V. E. *The doctor and the soul.* New York: Alfred A. Knopf, 1957.

Frankl, V. E. *Man's search for meaning: An introduction to logotherapy.* New York: Pocket Books, 1963.

Gendlin, E. T. *Focusing.* New York: Everest House, 1978.

Good news bible: The bible in today's English version. New York: American Bible Society, 1976.

The Holy Bible. King James version. New York: Harper & Brothers, 1951.

The Holy Bible. Revised standard version. New York: Oxford University Press, 1962.

Jacobson, E. *Progressive relaxation.* Chicago: The University of Chicago Press, 1974.

Jung, C. G. *Modern man in search of a soul.* New York: Harcourt, Brace, & World, 1933.

Kahn, H. I. *Spiritual dimensions of psychology.* Lebanon Springs, NY: Sufi Order Publications, 1981.

Maslow, A. H. *Religions, values, and peak-experiences.* New York: Viking, 1970.

Maultsby, M. C., Jr., & Ellis, A. *Technique for using rational-emotive imagery (REI).* New York: Institute for Rational Living, 1974.

Naranjo, C., & Ornstein, R. E. *On the psychology of meditation.* New York: Viking, 1971.

Parke, R. D. Punishment in children: Effects, side effects, and alternative strategies. In H. Holm & P. Robinson (Eds.), *Psychological processes in early education.* New York: Academic Press, 1977, pp. 71–97.

Perls, F. S. *The Gestalt approach and eye witness to therapy.* Palo Alto, CA: Science & Behavior Books, 1973.

Shorr, J. E. *Psychotherapy through imagery.* New York: Intercontinental Medical Book Corp., 1974.

Tart, C. T. (Ed.). *Transpersonal psychologies.* New York: Harper & Row, 1975.

Tillich, P. *Systematic theology.* Chicago: University of Chicago Press, 1957.

Walsh, R. N., & Vaughan, F. *Beyond ego: The transpersonal dimension in psychology.* Los Angeles: J. P. Tarcher, 1980.

Zeig, J. K. *Ericksonian psychotherapy* (Vol. 1 & 2). New York: Brunner/Mazel, 1985.

Chapter 8

HEALING FICTIONS

A Medieval Practice of Poetry Therapy*

Millicent Marcus

My textual sources are Giovanni Boccaccio's great philological compendium, *The Genealogy of the Gentile Gods,* and his *Decameron,* a collection of 100 short stories written in Florence in 1350, several years after the Black Plague of 1348, which wiped out two-thirds of the population of the city. The plague constitutes the framing situation, or what we call the "frame story" of the *Decameron,* in which seven young women and three young men gather in the church of Santa Maria Novella and decide to flee the pestilential city for the safety of the countryside outside Florence. They repair to a lovely villa where they can enjoy the good life, replete with wine, gourmet meals, and of course, servants. To wile away the time, they engage in courtly activities—singing, dancing, game-playing, and most importantly, storytelling. The young people tell tales for 10 days—hence the title *decameron: deca* is Greek for ten, and *meron* means days. Each

---

*Reprinted, by permission, from *An allegory of form: Literary self-consciousness in the 'Decameron'.* Stanford French and Italian Studies, *18,* Saratoga, CA: Anma Libri, 1979.

day's storytelling is governed by a different member of the group who serves as king or queen of the festivities and decides on a common theme for these tales told under his or her aegis. Thus, for example, Day Four is dedicated to stories of unhappy love, Day Seven to stories of how women cheat on their husbands, Day Ten to stories of generous and magnanimous deeds. The storytelling begins with the exploits of Ser Ciappelletto—a certified liar, swindler, murderer, thief, glutton, usurer, pederast, etc., who contracts the plague and on his deathbed gives the confession of a man of such unblemished virtue that he is taken for a saint and canonized.

The Church comes under repeated satiric attack in the *Decameron*. For example, when a monk is caught in bed with his ladylove, he seeks the pardon of his abbot who happens to be engaged in similar pleasurable pursuits of his own. Day Two features the tale of Alatiel who sets out on a voyage to meet her future husband, is kidnapped and carnally possessed by nine different men before being restored to her fiance who accepts her as his virgin bride. The first tale of Day Three tells of Masetto, a convent gardener, who ends up attending to the personal needs of all eight nuns and the abbess. Day Four is the one dedicated to tragic love. Here we read how Ghismonda is discovered *in flagrante delicto* by her father who cuts out her lover's heart and serves it to his daughter in a goblet. The Tenth and last Day is dedicated to tales of magnanimity. It is this day which "redeems" the human condition after so many tales of adultery, treachery, and practical jokes. Thus for example, Gentile dei Garisendi visits the crypt of the woman he loves (who happens to be married to another man) finds that she is not dead, revives her, restores her to health, and then returns the lady to her rightful husband. Now the 100 tales have been told and the frame-story youths leave their pastoral retreat to return to the city of Florence. And so ends the *Decameron*.

My theory about the *Decameron* is that storytelling, and fiction-making in general, is a healing process for Boccaccio. The *Decameron* is really poetry therapy writ large. I should preface this argument by saying that in the Middle Ages, poetry had a meaning far broader than it has for us moderns. It meant fiction-making itself, be it in prose or verse, as opposed to theological or philosophical discourse, or legal disputation. To quote Boccaccio's beautiful definition of poetry, "It brings forth strange unheard-of creations of the mind; it arranges these meditations in a fixed order, adorns the whole composition with unusual interweaving of words and thoughts and thus it veils truth in a fair and fitting garment of fiction."[1] I give special emphasis to this last phrase because it lies at the very heart of poetic theory in the Middle Ages. Medieval fictions were always allegorical—the literal level was made to point beyond itself to some hidden meaning. The interpretation of medieval texts is therefore a twofold process in which the letter is the "fictive veil" which must be pulled aside to reveal a deeper truth. Poetry thus exerts a double hold on the minds of its readers. If it is the sensuous pleasure of the poetic surface that first attracts us to a text, then it is the hidden treasures beneath the literal level which reward our prolonged study. The very effort which we must put into interpreting poetic meaning makes our discoveries that more precious. "What we acquire with difficulty and keep with care," said Boccaccio, "is always the dearer to us."[2]

Though the power and dignity of poetic creation seems obvious to us and should require no justification, Boccaccio, like many medieval writers, was often on the defensive. He had to defend his fiction-making not only against those who saw it as lewd and misleading, but against those who saw it as downright useless. "It is rather useful than damnable to compose stories," asserts Boccaccio, who goes on to include Jesus among the utilizers of poetic teaching devises.[3] But it is in the psychological benefits of fiction-making that Boccaccio's argument holds most interest for us in the present context. I'll let Boccaccio speak for himself on the subject. "Fiction . . . has been the means, as we often read, of quelling minds aroused to a mad rage, and subduing them to their pristine gentleness . . . By fiction, too, the strength and spirits of great men worn out in the strain of serious crises, have been restored. . . . One knows of princes who have been deeply engaged in important matters, but after the noble and happy disposal of their affairs of state, obey, as it were, the warning of nature and revive their spent forces by calling about them such men as will renew their weary minds with diverting stories and conversation. Fiction has, in some cases, sufficed to life the oppressive weight of adversity and furnish consolation."[4]

We are ready to return now to the *Decameron* and see how Boccaccio puts this notion of "healing fictions" into practice. He does so on several textual levels which lend themselves to the following schematization. On the outermost level, we have the author addressing a readership of idle, middle-class Florentine ladies who are kept in virtual seclusion by overprotective husbands, brothers, and fathers and who need the consolation of Boccaccio's stories. (This is the medieval equivalent of today's soap-opera public.) On the second level, we have the frame-story youths who leave the plague-ridden city to tell tales in the Tuscan countryside. Finally, we have the 100 tales themselves. On the outermost level, fictions work their healing powers on a Boccaccio caught in the throes of unrequited love. "While suffering this unhappiness," writes Boccaccio, "I was comforted by the pleasant talk and consolation of a friend, but for whom, I am firmly persuaded, I should now be dead."[5] Lest this sound like melodramatic exaggeration on Boccaccio's part, it should be recalled that in the Middle Ages, lovesickness was a certified medical syndrome with the physical and psychological symptoms that we today would associate with agitated depression. Furthermore, lovesickness was considered a terminal condition, unless alleviated by the lady's embraces or some other equivalent consolation. Thus, when Boccaccio says that he was saved from the clutches of death by the "pleasant talk" of a friend, we are to take him quite seriously, and to admire so wondrous a cure. Boccaccio never reveals the content of this therapeutic discourse, but goes on to say that he, in turn, plans to comfort fellow sufferers with stories. The suggestion is that the unspecified "pleasant talk," which cured him is really storytelling, and the unnamed friend is the spokesman for the storytelling legacy to which Boccaccio is heir. The *Decameron* will thus take its place in the cumulative tradition of healing through fiction, passing on to future readers the solace of these tales as they were received from a prior source.

The author's personal experience of remedial fictions is reflected on the next textual level by the example of the frame-story youths who flee the death-dealing city for a storytelling sojourn in the Tuscan countryside. Here, the lovesickness of the author is replaced by the indiscriminate destruction of the Black Plague; but the remedy is the same in both cases, regardless of the etiology or severity of the disease: storytelling. By positing the therapeutic effects of fiction-making, Boccaccio locates himself in a long and robust narrative tradition, whose most obvious example is the *Arabian Nights,* where Scheherazade tells a story every night in order to stave off the sultan's order for her execution. Storytelling literally keeps Scheherazade alive. In accordance with this tradition the frame-story youths' decision to leave the pestilential city and to tell tales makes storytelling tantamount to a redemption from death—poetry therapy writ large.

On the innermost level of the text, however, Boccaccio gives us examples of poetry therapy gone awry, where storytelling is used in ways which only worsen the malaise of the listeners. In the wrong hands, argues Boccaccio, the manipulative powers of poetry can be terribly abused and can heighten the collective pathology. This occurs most disturbingly on Day Four, where the theme is tales of tragic love. Filostrato, King for the day, proposes this theme because it best reflects his own woebegone state as a victim of unrequited passion. "It is my pleasure" announced Filostrato, "that we tell tales on a theme in conformity with my own fate . . . that is, about persons whose love ended unhappily."[6] He wants stories told under his reign which would mirror his own miserable condition, allowing him to wallow in self-pity and dramatize his plight to the world. But the other frame-story youths rebel against Filostrato's pathological fiction-making and, once Day Four is over, they hasten to restore the constructive, comic mood of the *Decameron.* The tendency to maudlin, narcissistic fiction-making must be exorcized if truly healing poetic mode is to be found. Boccaccio's other 9 storytelling days offer that therapeutic corrective.

At the end of the *Decameron,* Boccaccio's frame-story youths return to the plague-ravaged city. It is this bold act of social reentry which perhaps best proves the power of Boccaccio's restorative fictions. In the wake of unspeakable destruction and loss, these young people have reaffirmed the regenerative capacity of the human imagination. "The poet," said Boccaccio, "is the creator who fashions a new world of nature and of man in all their phases and activities, and so manipulates the illusion of this new world as to capture and control the minds of his hearers."[7] In its testimony to man's imaginative resilience in the face of collective disaster, Boccaccio's *Decameron* offers convincing proof that poetry therapy may indeed be the very elixir of life.

REFERENCES

1. *Boccaccio on poetry, being the preface and the fourteenth and fifteenth books of Boccaccio's 'Genealogia Deorum Gentilium,'*, C. G. Osgood, (trans.). Indianapolis and New York: Bobbs Merrill, 1956, p. xxxv. [Emphases added.]

2. *Ibid,* p. 62.

3. *Ibid,* p. 47.

4. *Ibid,* p. 50.

5. *The Decameron of Giovanni Boccaccio,* R. Aldington, (trans.). New York: Dell, 1974, p. 25.

6. *Ibid,* p. 241. [Emphases are my own.]

7. *Boccaccio on poetry,* p. xxxvl.

Chapter 9

POETRY AS THERAPY WITH HANDICAPPED ADOLESCENTS

Theresa G. Morrison

Alone, Alone, Alone
What does it mean to be alone?
To have no girl friend?
No confidence in myself?
To live without hope?
I am alone.
It's overpowering my mind
Driving me crazy
There is a being in me
That works on me
How can I get rid of it
Alone, Alone, Alone
Is there no hope
I can hear only the sound
Of the world's loneliness
Now it's reaching to devour me
My heart beats louder
Alone, Alone
Every heartbeat tells me

I am alone
Some crazy thing has taken control
And the worst is yet to come.

This poem was written by Kim,* an eighteen-year-old Chinese-American boy, when he was attending a series of sessions in poetry therapy at the High School Homebound Program of the Federation of the Handicapped. Until the age of five, Kim had never spoken at all. After that, both at home and outside, he found it difficult and frustrating to make his feelings known. These frustrations led to violent and disordered behavior, and at the age of eight he was committed to a mental hospital. At the time of his commitment, the diagnosis was "chronic brain syndrome, associated with behavioral problems." The staff judged him to be "hostile, suspicious, uncooperative, hyperactive, and practically mute." Three years later he was discharged, having been found to be of normal intelligence with no evidence of psychosis. He was then eleven years old but unable to adjust to the regular school program. He was transferred to the home instruction program, and in the junior year of high school was recommended for and accepted into the Federation program. The supervising psychiatrist's data noted Kim's hostility, his depressed self-image, his anxiety, and sense of incompetence.

Kim could not make himself understood except through written notes. His speech impairment was traced to "congenital suprabulbar palsy" which impeded talk and caused him to drool. He managed to function acceptably on the academic program and showed special interest in the paid-work feature of the vocational program. However, he refused to accept therapy, would not keep his appointments with the staff psychologist, and remained apart from the other students. He was invited to attend the poetry therapy group which assembled Friday afternoons for 90-minute sessions.

The group of 12 students would meet around a table located in the workshop. Kim would position himself in a corner behind a large steel cabinet out of view of the group, silent but able to

---

*All names in this chapter are fictional.

listen to the proceedings. It was at our fourth meeting that he handed the counselor his poem, *Alone*. Still in concealment, he heard his contribution read and discussed by his classmates. He heard members of the group describing their own feelings of social isolation, "norm"-lessness, and powerlessness. They were expressing the same fears and self-doubts that were the subject of his poem and spoke with respect of the writer.

For the next two sessions Kim clung to his retreat. But one Friday afternoon he took his place with the other students. He became prolific in his writing and, in spite of his impaired speech and its attendant drooling, he initiated conversations with group members.

He began to seek out the rehabilitation counselor, bringing his poems and his confidences. In discussions with the counselor, the pattern of his past life evolved. It seemed that the Chinese community of which he was a part was exceptionally status-conscious and unsympathetic to the handicapped. His grandfather had told him that it would have been better if he had not been born since no woman would ever want to marry him.

At this point, Kim agreed to hospitalization for a corrective operation on his palate and pharynx. His speech improved, and this led to increased socialization and better rapport with the staff, whom he surprised with his talkativeness and gregariousness. He spelled out verbally the words he couldn't pronounce, and no longer became angry when he failed to make himself understood. He could be reasoned with.

One day he brought some records to one of our parties. When he found that one had been taken, he kicked the furniture, banged doors, threw books wildly across the room, yelled words that seemed meaningless, and sounded like an animal in pain. It was a repetition of the behavior he had exhibited at home, and of which his family had complained. Yet we now could reason with him. We explained that there were better ways to handle anger. This scene was never repeated again at this agency.

It was in his senior year that Kim felt that gymnasium space should be alloted to the boys in the program. Having discussed this with the counselor, he helped to draw up a list of community facilities where cooperation could be sought. Accompanied by one of the college interns assisting the staff, he visited a neighborhood church, a school, and a branch of the Salvation Army. The Salvation Army agreed to set aside certain designated hours for the use of their gym by the students. On our office blackboard after this victory, Kim wrote, "We deserve."

From a youth who had been inactive, late, at times violent, isolated, and nonaccepting of therapy, he had progressed to one who could socialize with others, devise and put into operation a strategy for the common good, and then follow it through to a successful conclusion.

At graduation Kim was voted the citation as the student who had made the greatest progress. During his senior year it was noted that he could hold a part-time job in a supermarket, could accept supervision, and could perform responsibly. Having passed an examination for an entry-level civil service job, and while waiting for an appointment, Kim registered in a special program offered by the Board of Education for the speech-impaired.

Kim has remained in touch with the agency. We were informed that he received his appointment, passed the probationary period, likes his work, and looks forward someday to a happy marriage.

The unpredictability of the areas into which a poem may lead is one of the special virtues of poetry therapy. By reaching into pockets of hurt and resentment and bringing into the open significant material that surfaces during these sessions, it facilitates progress in treatment. In the judgment of the supervising psychiatrist at our agency, the poetry therapy sessions make possible "important observations and insights which might have been missed by the clinicians."

A poem by Edwin Markham, dealing with social ostracism, prompted a flood of autobiographical outpourings from our students.

Outwitted

He drew a circle that shut me out
Heretic, rebel, a thing to flout.
But love and I had the wit to win
We drew a circle that took him in.[1]

Lisette, whose reputation for snobbery had drawn its own circle around her, was shocked to learn in the course of the discussion that followed a reading of the poem that, while she was desperate for acceptance, something unapproachable in her manner had kept the others from her. It was touching to observe how readily they were prepared to offer their reassurance when they were made aware of her true feelings.

An attractive teenager then disclosed an experience she had previously found too painful to discuss with anyone, even in private therapy sessions. She had been blackballed from a sorority by girls she had believed were her friends. She spoke of her anguish. "The whole thing," she recalled, "turned me off people. It ruined me. I felt I could never again trust anyone." This fact, when reported to her psychologist, proved to bear importantly on the progress of her therapy.

At the following session, Anne, a black girl, who had for years been subject to attacks of asthma and who also suffered from a severe eczema which she aggravated by compulsive scratching, submitted the following poem:

Prejudice

Prejudice is the love one bears
His own people
That causes him to spit
On beautiful innocent victims
Of another race

Prejudice is a force
That prevents two people from saying
"Hey, I love you"!

Prejudice is an ache
Surrounding my heart,
Making it feel
About to drop
Into the pit of hell.

Anne had been unable to benefit from attendance in regular classes at school because of her rebellion at authority. Up to this point she remained uncooperative with staff members, refusing guidance and balking at supervision. During her individual therapy sessions she was taciturn and exhibited resentment. However, the sympathetic reception given her poem by the group encouraged her to compose new ones. She participated more actively in the following sessions, sharing her problems with the group. She spoke of how it felt to be a member of a black family in a middle-class white neighborhood. She was able to discuss her ambivalence in racial matters. She wanted to be like the white people among whom she lived but hated them for their rejection of her. For Anne the poetry therapy sessions provided a useful emotional outlet, an escape hatch for her confused feelings and a forum where she could express her opinions and thoughts to an understanding audience.

Her therapist commented that Anne had grown more communicative. She was not as resistant to guidance and accepted our suggestions for vocational counseling and placement. She has her high school diploma, works during the day and attends evening classes at a college. She continues to make periodic visits to the Federation and reports on her progress. Her attacks of asthma have been reduced, and her eczema has receded. She enjoys her job and is doing well in her studies.

At our case conferences, attended by the supervising psychiatrist, the coordinator, the psychologists, the vocational counselor, the workshop evaluator, and the counselor acting as poetry therapist, material relevant to further guidance and vocational exploration gleaned from the poetry sessions is reviewed in the context of planning further treatment.

Outwitted never fails to elicit a lively response. There are also a number of poets, especially those who have themselves struggled with serious mental problems, who also make a strong appeal to our students. These include Robert Frost, Emily Dickinson, William Blake, William Wordsworth, Theodore Roethke. The list is long of the many others who have made for lively encounters: Denise Levertov, Gwendolyn Brooks, Langston Hughes, Countee Cullen, Walt Whitman, and Louise Bogan are among them. Interestingly enough, some nineteenth century poets such as Shelley, Keats, and Browning, are equally effective.

After a reading of John Keats's sonnet, *When I Have Fears That I May Cease to Be*, the seemingly irresponsible youthful group wrestled with such profundities as reincarnation, compensation, and the nature of good and evil, as well as their hitherto unexpressed fears of dying. A student who acknowledged that he had for a long time been haunted by a dread of premature death, found reassurance in the disclosures of other students that they had similar fears. It came as a surprise to the counselor as well as to the group members to discover how many of those handicapped believe that their affliction in this life is an atonement for evil committed in an earlier incarnation. It became possible for the counselor to explore this notion as a misconception.

This same session triggered a reaction in one of the participants. Rosa, a bright and pretty young girl diagnosed as schizophrenic, had consistently identified herself with animals. When speaking she would strike an attitude, lifting her hands in front of her face to resemble paws. Her features would set in imitation of the expression of a dog. She would make animal sounds and preface her statements with "My dog would say—" or "My dog would feel—." She avoided relating as a human being. She would frequently repeat, "Dogs are nicer than people. They are never nasty." She was a gifted artist, and her notebooks were filled with animal drawings. She refused to draw humans.

In the discussion that followed the reading of Keats's poem someone asked the question: "What kind of person would return to life as a thorn?" Rosa volunteered that it would be someone who needed thorns for protection. And then she added, "My name is Rosa, I am a rose that has thorns." This was the first time she associated herself with anything other than an animal. To her therapist this new identification was charged with significance.

We provided thermofax copies of poems to the group. A lyric by Madeline Mason was the focus of our attention the week following the reading of the poem by John Keats.

My Mother Wept

My mother wept
And when I asked her why?
She gave no answer
Only shook her head.

Now I,
The years upon me,
As they were not then,
Know why
Her tears were shed.

Memory-laden,
My mother wept,
Now I,
Heavy with my own tears,
Cry.[2]

In the margin of her copy where she would customarily doodle dogs in various attitudes, Rosa this time drew a picture of a mother and child. Shortly afterwards she handed in the following poem entitled *The Spasm:*

I once wrote a silly poem
About a guy I liked.
Was it lust
Or the soaring feeling of a gliding Gull
I tried to express?
My mother shown that poem
revealed her empty opinion,
And I felt ashamed.
Months later
I found that scrap of paper
In which I had put in too much
    feeling
And I was overcome

By a spasm
Of shame remembered.

Experience with students in our poetry program tends to confirm a statement by Robert E. Jones, M.D., director of the Institute of the Pennsylvania Hospital: "Adolescents have more poetry in their lives than any segment of the population other than English professors . . . adolescents entering mental hospitals bring with them the normal interest in poetic form. It may even be that nervous adolescents have a more intense interest in poetic forms than their better adjusted peers."[3]

In one of the many poems that followed the first *Alone,* Kim wrote, "I stand apart and whisper to your image in my heart." A schizophrenic girl, describing aging, said, "It creeps crawling then strikes with the inimitable force of snow." In a poem, *Love Me,* another lonely teenager pleaded, "Grasp my life-giving hands. Hold my mind tenderly."

Albert Rothenberg, M.D., associate professor of psychiatry at the Yale School of Medicine in *Psychiatry,* August 1972, affirmed, "Poets and psychiatrists are blood brothers."[4] "The poet," wrote John Dewey, "has an immense advantage over even the psychologist in dealing with an emotion. For the former builds up a concrete situation and permits it to evoke emotional response."[5] Instead of a description of an emotion in intellectual and symbolic terms. The artist "does the deed that breeds the emotion."

"In poetry," suggests Helen Vendler, professor of English at Boston University, "the hungry adolescent can find all the truths of feeling that the schools and his parents are afraid to tell him. Truths about anger, chagrin, grief, yearning, self-consciousness, and despair." The young need it most, she believes, "in order to sort out and make sense of their emotions, to be reassured that their hidden feelings are not obscure and shameful private disease."[6]

Included in Dr. Leedy's *Poetry Therapy* is this poem by a homebound student composed as a tribute to the therapeutic magic of poetry.

To Poetry*

You shine on my bitter days
Like a sky full of stars

---

*Reprinted, by permission, from Poetry therapy with disturbed adolescents (Morrison). In J. J. Leedy (Ed.), *Poetry therapy: The use of poetry in the treatment of emotional disorders.* Philadelphia: J. B. Lippincott & Co., 1969.

Like the sun who breaks his arrows
On a dark river.

My beloved poetry

Folds my soul in blue elements
So that I can be water,
Tempest, or flame.

REFERENCES

1. Markham, E. Outwitted. In L. Untermer (Ed.), *Modern American poetry*. New York: Harcourt Brace and Company, 1962, p. 106.

2. Mason, M. My mother wept. Unpublished poem. Reprinted by permission from Madeline Mason, February 24, 1986.

3. Jones, R. The double door. In J. J. Leedy, (Ed.), *Poetry therapy: The use of poetry in the treatment of emotional disorders*. Philadelphia: Lippincott, 1969.

4. Rothenberg, A. Poetic process and psychotherapy. *Psychiatry,* August 1972, p. 238.

5. Dewey, J., *Art as experience*. New York: Capricorn Books, 1958, p. 15.

6. Vendler, H., *New York Times Book Review,* October 15, 1972, p. 3.

Chapter 10

POEMS AND HYMN TUNES AS SONGS

Creative Therapy, or "Innocent Merriment"?

Joseph Jones

When words join music there is reenacted the process by which poetry is thought to have been born. Modern song may differ radically from ancient hymn or saga, both in form and content, and the audience may be single or vastly plural (as also at times in the past), but it would be difficult to believe that the experience both of singing and of hearing song has value only as idle entertainment. The church hymn is one of the commonest examples of song which invites a pleasurable response and at the same time (for many if not necessarily all the singers) an intellectual one as well.

Rather unexpectedly, one of the warmest tributes to hymn singing comes from the pen of Mark Twain, who was less than enthusiastic about much religious experience of his day. In *Huckleberry Finn* the "king" has just finished a lugubrious fit of sorrow, impersonating the brother and heir of Peter Wilks,

> And the minute the words were out of his mouth
> somebody over in the crowd struck up the doxolojer, and
> everybody joined in with all their might, and it just warmed
> you up and made you feel as good as church letting out.

128

> Music *is* a good thing; and after all that soul-butter and
> hogwash I never see it freshen up things so, and sound so
> honest and bully.[1]

Mark Twain describes here what technically may be termed
therapy: out of music of many kinds comes abundant evidence
of tension-relieving, healing powers.

These preliminary remarks are related to a 15-minute sample of songs made from secular poems set to hymn tunes; these
songs were selected from *Poems and Hymn Tunes*[2] which includes
poem-songs by Romantic poets (Byron, Coleridge, Shelley, Pea-
cock, Hogg), later nineteenth-century poets such as Browning,
Tennyson, Landor, Hopkins; and much earlier British figures,
e.g. Wyatt, Marlowe, Raleigh, Shakespeare, Jonson, Donne,
Herrick, Marvell, Suckling, and Wither. Among North Americans are Poe, Longfellow, Emerson, Whitman, Dickinson, Tho-
reau, Lampman (Canadian), and H. H. Brownell.

The practice of setting poems to music is of course not new[3],
although it is undertaken more often by professional composers
than by persons (like myself) with no more than run-of-the-mill
musical ability. It requires exploration, integration, and affirmation. Manipulative skills, called into play to match melody with
meter, may range from simple searching to highly complex in-
vention. The kind of *exploration* needed for combining poems
with hymn tunes would fall well towards the lower end of the
scale, especially when it is remembered that most hymnals are
open to fairly rapid search by virtue of their metrical indexes.
A ballad-stanza poem fits readily with a common meter tune; so
the *integration* is one of known with known, though the song thus
produced has at least a little claim to novelty. By *affirmation* I
mean achieving finally, perhaps after considerable trial and error,
a feeling that the song *is* singable and may please an audience.
Otherwise, the search had better be abandoned and some other
combination attempted.

For the maker of this kind of song (I use "maker" as a relatively neutral term between "arranger" and "composer"), a variety of results is possible. Literature students and teachers, for
instance, will find that metrics take on a directly functional
meaning as seen and used to match poem and tune. Making and

singing songs can be a useful learning aid. One's perceptions of differences between old and new diction in the poems chosen will extend, gradually, to the styles of the tunes, which range all the way from ancient plainsong to new melodies from our own century. (My personal preferences, together with copyright limitations on recent poems and tunes, limit me to a cutoff date no later than about 1875.) Use of a number of different hymnals as sourcebooks can make one aware of period preferences among certain hymns as well as of solid continuity among others. No two religious denominations are likely to exhibit extensive agreement as to what to put into their hymnals; some differ very widely indeed; yet a few hymns are all but universally used and cherished. Computerization of the metrical indexes to, let us say, several dozen of the most widely available contemporary hymnals and their earlier editions would probably render the searching process considerably easier, but less challenging and enjoyable. One mechanical improvement of recent years, already indispensable, is the high-grade copying machine, especially the kind that enlarges and reduces. In short, there is more than enough to do—pleasant work for the most part—to help feed creative urgings.

For the hearer, there is the attraction of something new, simple and easy as it may appear to be (but it isn't invariably easy to come up with something readily singable). It is nearly always stimulating to observe old matter in a fresh context, and that applies both to the poems and the tunes. One finds it hard to believe, until he hears for himself, how different—and assuasive—a tune and/or poem can be in a new combination.

Hymnology stands, ultimately, to gain from what might at first seem a raid upon its territory. An interest in tunes for new secular words could result, in some hands, in new religious words as well. It must be apparent to many users of hymnals that dozens of the "poems" to which the tunes are fitted (sometimes not very skillfully) are woefully out of date if in fact they ever were "good poetry" as against merely "good theology." Too often, attractive tunes have helped keep alive mediocre words which it is long past time to abandon. Once separated (not to say liberated), the tune has some chance, at least, of finding more acceptable religious lyrics. Nor must we forget that by no means are all hymn tunes of genuinely, purely religious origin: folksongs, borrowings from symphonic or operatic composers, miscellaneous traditional melodies—all were incorporated at times into hymnals. In their time, such tunes must no doubt have seemed novel enough to raise eyebrows in some congregations.

Secular uses outnumber religious, and offer considerable variety. Programs of song, for instance, may be easily arranged, as well as combinations with spoken poetry and with other performing arts. Depending upon the type and complexity of song, all the usual voice arrangements—solo, solo and chorus, duet, quartet, etc.—will be called into play. Accompaniments, likewise, may range from piano or accordion to guitar, banjo, or autoharp. Special poetic forms such as the sonnet or free verse can be accommodated. Not to be overlooked is the emergence, upon occasion, of original verse generated by some part of the process. There is good possibility, given continuing activity by numerous experimenters, of something new and rare.

The poet Virgil is reported to have said, "Do not commit your poems to pages alone: sing them, I pray you." This advice is still good today—not for every poem, to be sure, but for quite a surprising number. And poetic song commonly affords Portia's double blessing upon giver and taker alike, upon maker-performer and audience.

REFERENCES

1. Twain, M. *Huckleberry Finn.* New York: Dodd, 1984.

2. Jones, J. *Poems and hymn tunes as songs: Metrical partners* (A manual with cassettes.). Guilford, CT: Jeffrey Norton Publishers, 1984.

3. Jones, J. Vom hymnal hoch: or, How to fashion new songs out of old segments. *Christianity and Literature,* (Summer 1982) *32*(4), 13–18.

Chapter 11

ANOTHER ROYAL ROAD

Frances Cappon Geer

One of my most fascinating cases began at Queensborough Community College in 1971 when I was counseling a newly returned Vietnam veteran. The turning point of the case occurred at a crisis, when the therapy turned into poetry therapy. The client describes the power of this change in the following words: "Writing a poem is like being seized by a seizure. Something takes their nails and scratches me deeply and draws blood. That blood is my words." Before going on, I wish to say a word about my personal experience as a therapist and what I think I have learned about the inner poetic voice.

I feel in a specially privileged position to be able to hear what is in someone's heart. Often I feel that a client is speaking to me from some deep creative source. He seems to be developing a special art form flowing from an inner identity. I am in effect an audience of one, listening to and witnessing an evolving self. At times I feel invited to respond and even to blend with what is occurring. Something universal as well as most private is happening. The spontaneous poetry of a session is like a butterfly which darts around and disappears so quickly that it rarely has a chance to be caught or examined as art.

In contacting a patient's innermost process, I believe the therapist is close to the symbol and metaphor factory. This may be a literal treasure chest. My job is to catch the metaphor, hold on to it firmly with my memory, and pass it back to the client at the right moment; for that symbol is the secret of his growth.

The sense of where the metaphors are manufactured came when I was counseling the client I mentioned, the Vietnam veteran who wanted to control his violent rages. He was a macho Marine, or "Marine-machine" as he came to label himself later. He had learned throughout life to keep his feelings bottled up until the pressure got so great they exploded. His parents nicknamed him "Crazy Billy." They feared for him, because they never knew what he was going to do next.

As I counseled him, he spoke quite fluently and always seemed to be in control; that is, until he got in touch with his feelings. Then all at once he would be silent and look around the room with his eyes very wide open. His eyes, intensely blue, contrasted with his dark hair and beard. He would stand up suddenly, grab his chest and stagger across my office mumbling something incomprehensible, and then collapse on some pillows next to the wall. The first time this happened I was very alarmed. He groaned from his position on the floor. I dared not leave him in this state. I watched him closely, looking for a signal of some kind.

He lifted his hand ever so slightly to beckon me. I knelt on the floor and took his hand. I could feel a slight pressure. I asked him if he was all right and could talk. He nodded and mumbled something about falling into the sea and finding strange creatures all around. I encouraged him to look around under the sea and tell me what was happening. He spoke of being afraid of the creatures. I encouraged him to continue making his way along the ocean floor, and to befriend the creatures. As we worked in this way, I seemed to be joining him on a weird journey.

After about 20 minutes he awakened and was perfectly normal again. He looked at me with surprise and asked: "What happened?" I stared back, feeling a little stupid. I think he interpreted my puzzled silence as secret wisdom about some mysterious process. There had been similar moments in Vietnam when he blacked out and woke up later; but the doctor could find no explanation for them.

Falling into these almost enchanted trances became a frequent event in our sessions. I must say that I never felt secure when they happened; in fact I tried to conduct the sessions so that they would not, but I could never figure out quite how. Nevertheless, each time I took the journey that they presented, I talked him through the nightmarish state. The journeys, all different, at times seemed mythical. I couldn't take notes; he always reached out for my hand in his fear, as he slipped into some kind of creative stupor or twilight zone.

Five years later he came to see me again. He was severely depressed and in psychic pain. When we got close to his feelings he seemed on the verge of violence toward himself. He raised his fist as if to smash it into the wall or against the floor. Once he came close to putting his fist through the window saying: "If I thought it would help, I would put this fist right through the window." My job was to go slowly and to help him survive these attacks of self-hate. In spite of my caution I would sometimes touch such a sensitive area that he would fall into one of his trances. I worried specially about these trances because these stressful visions were now accompanied by physical pain. I urged him to see a doctor for a checkup. Because of his frequent impulse to pound a wall, and now these physically painful trances, I felt that I was walking a tightrope; I feared potential confrontations.

I could go into the content of what was happening in his life—such as having a very unsatisfying job involving a kind of frenzied physical labor, and the lack of any real personal relationships; but I believe this would be superficial. The real work that had to be done was somewhere in the trances and the fury of his impulses toward self-punishment. He refused to look at his childhood, or at his experiences in Vietnam and even resisted talking about the present.

One day, as he was speaking about death, I rapidly took down his words as he spoke. Writing them down gave me a new perspective and all at once I felt their beauty. "Let me read something to you." I said. When I finished he looked at me in amazement and asked: "Who wrote that?" "You did," I answered, "and it sounds like a poem to me." He could hardly believe that I was reading his own words back to him. He wondered if he could take my notes home. I said, "of course. These words belong to you."

In each following session, as I wrote, he would ask for my notes. He had spoken forth a spontaneous poem for me to hear and I gave it back to him in scribbled form. It was a ceremony—an exchange of gifts. I regret that I could never make copies of those poems. There was no time. It was important to give him immediate feedback on what was taking place. He could possess his words; reading them was like getting acquainted with his inner self. In the course of our ceremony he discovered his poetic voice and before long he was bringing me presents in return—his completed, usually just memorized, poems about the things we could never talk about directly.

In some way each patient teaches you how to be his therapist and I realized he needed me to be grateful and full of praise. Later he chided me, saying he valued other people's opinions more because they were critical. But, he added, he didn't think he could take it if I were critical, because the poems were his scars. He learned to protect his poems from the uncaring. I continued the gift-giving ceremony by typing each poem and our discussions of their meanings, giving him a copy and keeping one for myself.

My gratitude and praise were fulfilling a real need. I believe I was performing the function of a mirror in Kohut's sense, that so important phase in a child's early years when he is praised by his mother and in the process develops a strong sense of self. His own mother had tried to terminate her pregnancy and later told my client in detail about how she had tried to kill him before he was born. So painful is this area that he would almost always collapse into a trance when I inquired into those early years.

His poems over the past 2 years trace the stages of his journey. In the beginning his poems were about rage, Vietnam, and death wishes. One poem, "Suicide Slide and . . ." was a description of a suicide attempt. The poem in effect was saying to the powers that be: "If you are not going to release me from this madness, release me to death." He struggled with this thought, while sitting at night on the beach, his poetic habitat. He stared deeply at the darkening ocean holding a razor in his hand. Fortunately, he went back into his cabin for something and heard the telephone ringing. I had received his urgent message but hadn't been able to reach him until that moment. Luckily we could talk.

His poetry gave us an opportunity to talk about things formerly taboo. Poetry dramatically changed his therapy. By confronting his inner demons through poetry he could avoid the trances. Gradually, he turned his back on the magnetic pull of death and reached out for life.

Nine months ago the doctors examined my client and told him that he had a prolapsed valve, and that he needed to have an arteriogram of his heart which would involve a procedure that would take 3 days in the hospital. Before the exam he went down to the beach and stared at the waves but this time wishing to live. The ocean felt like the source of life. The next day he went into the hospital. When they wheeled him into the operating room, he asked the nurse for some paper and a pencil so he could write. She said: "You can't do that in here." Instead, he created the poem in his mind. During the procedure there was an emergency when his pulse dropped. Doctors in a flurry of activity gave him the impression that his life was ebbing away. Later when he was moved back to his hospital room he wrote the poem "Angiogram".*

> Mortality. . . Reality
> Still another minute please
> Dust to dust . . . well enough
> Still *another* minute please
> Death's blissful bliss . . . like a kiss
> Still another minute please
> Soft surrender . . . womb like remember
> Still another minute please

Incredibly, he had never read or written any poems. He came from an uneducated immigrant family and received a legacy of street wisdom. He pointed out in a recent session that he could easily have become a con man but that now he wanted to make a contribution to the world. In spite of his background, a poet

---

*Quoted by permission of my client, who reserves all other publication rights.

was born. I say poet because, for the past 2 years or so, writing poems has become a way of life. He said after the arteriogram: "I shall never stop writing poetry."

But what was this magic—as it did seem to me? I believe that the trances were somehow transformed into works of art. Through his poetry, symbols were formed that served as anchors of meaning for his pain. This creative process introduced him to his inner self and the aliveness of his Being. At the same time it externalized his violent feelings in the form of poems that we could examine together and thereby gain greater control over his violent impulses. Accordingly, it gave him an ever increasing power of choice on how to behave. The inner demons came to hold hands with angels, as he put it in one of his poems. Recording his feelings as poems gave them an existence and a value outside himself. In effect, he created something of potential value first for his therapist and then for people in general. It is with his permission that I have prepared a selection of his poetry in the form of a pamphlet entitled, *A Vietnam Veteran Speaks: A Journey Through the Mask via Poetry.*

What was my role in the birth of this poet? I merely wrote down his words—words that he in fact did not recognize until I said they belonged to him. I had given form to the pain flowing from his psyche and made it tangible. In this way he could possess his pain in symbolic form, and turn it into a pearl, as he once observed. I performed the ego work that the poet would ordinarily do himself. I did not initiate a process in this patient. I took advantage of a process that was already there, flowing out from deeper levels of consciousness and unconsciousness with its ambiguities and multiple meanings. My gift to the patient was a return of the patient's self, something the patient had lost and needed to have returned. My gift enabled an expansion of trust, because the creation of the poem also gave value to my Being for him.

When I wrote the article *Marine Machine to Poet of the Rocks* I gave it to my client to read and to get his reaction and possible suggestions. I also wanted to ask his permission for possible publication. He told me that he read the article and rejoiced. Later he confessed that he often read it at night when he was alone and got comfort from it. When the article was accepted by *The*

Arts in Psychotherapy, I asked him how he felt about some of his poems being published. He said: "Words are my scars. Somehow, something will be missed. The reader gets the resultant mark, but not the pain as process. The poem is insufficient to convey that." He went on to describe his poetic process: "A battle rages that accurately calls for the words that depict the struggle. The struggle is slow. When you are trying to call forth the words, it seems as if you are in mortal combat. The words are resisting wildly not to be called forth. They are being taken from the darkness of the unconscious. You are casting light on them and they resist that light. The dark forces of evil die when they meet the light."

To sum up briefly: when I saw my client in 1981 he was depressed to the point of being suicidal. He had difficulty keeping a job or making any commitments and he was isolated and withdrawn. Today he has been working for over a year as a manager in a union where he is highly regarded. During the past year he successfully organized a sit-in strike of veterans who were trying to get more help from their Center. Through his leadership and negotiations with a director from Washington, he was able to get through some important reforms in the operation of the Center, and was commended by the national director. In addition, my client is making more personal connections with fellow veterans and reaching out toward greater and more realistic intimacy with women. But even more important than these somewhat external signs, he wants to live and to make some positive contribution to the world.

Poetry therapists talk of reading or writing poetry as a therapeutic experience, but in this case it is also finding poetry in the therapeutic experience. Every patient is a poet to some extent. To be a good therapist one must be a poet too, or at least be able to hear the poetry.

My client's trances, which some might judge to be possible schizophrenic episodes, were given form and structure and thereby made less ego-alien. What could have been a potentially destructive experience was changed into a self-creative experience for therapeutic growth. Offering support and safety and integrative friendliness toward the threatening forces helped to give control over the shadow of the demonic.

The creative part of the mind that abstracts symbols may

well also be the place where therapeutic change occurs. In other words, meaningful therapy and creative art come from the same source. Perhaps the artist has discovered that being creative lifts him out of a depression—A valuable result if it weren't for the next stage of vulnerability to criticism, which could bring him abruptly down from the "high."

The artist may be someone especially sensitive or prone to pathology from the beginning. Instead of going to a therapist perhaps he tries to cure himself through art. From observing his enthusiasm, one might wonder whether he has found a pleasure trigger in his brain. Conceivably, this pleasure trigger is the very edge where artistic and therapeutic change takes place. But why isn't the artist usually happy? Unfortunately, if he is to make a living, the artist must be geared to social approval. Not finding it could swing him to the depressive stage. The patient in therapy has the advantage because he has a therapist who can be his accepting audience.

The reason that approval is so important both to the artist and to the patient is that both are producing feelings and thoughts that expose a very sensitive inner self, pleasurefully growing as a result of the process, but unprotected by the usual mask. In conclusion I believe that both therapy and art spring from and nurture the growth of the self, which is an interesting paradox; the growth of the self generates what it both seeks and is. Ideally, the process should be a pleasure.

BIBLIOGRAPHY

Ansell, C. Psychoanalysis and poetry. In A. Lerner (Ed.), *Poetry in the therapeutic experience*. New York: Pergamon Press, 1978 (pp. 12–23).

Blanton, S. *The healing power of poetry*. New York: Crowell, 1960.

Geer, F. Guided fantasy with a giant doll. *Voices*, 1978, *14*, 81–84.

Geer, F. Bernardino's portrait, art therapy as an existential technique: A counselor's painting leads into a deeper picture of the client. *Voices*, 1982, *17*, 43–50.

Geer, F. Marine-machine to poet of the rocks: Poetry therapy as a bridge to inner reality: Some exploratory observations. *The Arts in Psychotherapy*, 1983, *10*, 9–14.

Geer, F. (Ed.) A Vietnam veteran speaks, a journey through the mask via poetry. Unpublished manuscript, 1984.

Howard, S. The Vietnam warrior: His experience and implications for psychotherapy. *American Journal of Psychotherapy*, 1976, *30*, 121–135.

Kohut, H. *The analysis of the self*. New York: International Universities Press, 1971.

Kohut, H. *The restoration of the self*. New York: International Universities Press, 1977.

Leedy, J. J. (Ed.) *Poetry therapy: The use of poetry in the treatment of emotional disorders*. Philadelphia: Lippincott, 1969.

Leedy, J. J. (Ed.) *Poetry the healer*. Philadelphia: Lippincott, 1973.

Niederland, G. W., & Sholevar, B. The creative process—A psychoanalytic discussion. *The Arts in Psychotherapy*, 1981, *8*, 71–101.

Shatan, C. F. The grief of soldiers. *American Journal of Orthopsychiatry*, 1973, *43*, 640–653.

Chapter 12

REFLECTIONS OF THOSE WHO SURVIVED

(The Bataan Death March)*

Nene Sims Glenn

In early 1942, the Philippines became the site of a harsh lesson in endurance for thousands of American soldiers. Forced to retreat before the furious onslaught of the Japanese Army, the American forces were ordered by MacArthur to withdraw to the rugged Bataan Peninsula and there fight the final defensive battle against the invading Japanese troops. Unfortunately, the exhausted men found that sufficient supplies had not been moved to accommodate them. As a result, the defending army found itself fighting not only the Japanese soldiers but also a losing battle against starvation and illness. Surrounded by starving and sick men, General King surrendered his forces on Bataan April 9, 1942, in order to prevent the useless spilling of more

---

*While researching for her thesis, the author found a list of the survivors of the "Bataan Death March." Correspondence with these survivors provided the material for this chapter. Some survivors sent diaries or details of events; others sent poetry written on bits of paper or small notepads. Thus this chapter researches the experiences of a large number of the survivors rather than the events of a single survivor.

blood for an already lost cause. Instead of finding themselves removed from any further conflict by the surrender, the weary soldiers found themselves beginning their hardest battle of all—the struggle for life. The victorious Japanese evacuated the defeated men to prisoner of war camps in what has become the infamous "Bataan Death March." During this horrible, dehumanizing trek, the Americans faced thirst, hunger, exhaustion, illness, and the brutality of the Japanese guards in such degree that one out of every five men died. To survive this and the ensuing months of harsh captivity, the Americans individually and collectively had to find ways of coping with their misfortunes. Some turned to God for hope and comfort; others found hidden resources within themselves; still others turned to poetry or humor, finding the written word a soothing balm to their tragedies and sufferings.

> Out of Bataan and the jungle Hell,
> Through crimson fields where comrades fell
> Along the dark road, stained with red
> Life's blood from our scattered dead,
> Who fought and starved to hold Bataan,
> Moved captives now in caravan.
>
> A caravan by Fate prepared,
> On journey dark by friends declared
> For captured men whom Death had spared,
> To feel the knuckles of her bony hand,
> When yellow typhoons racked Bataan,
> And captives now in caravan.
>
> Through windblown mountains' deep
>   ravine,
> Where lay the slain, not yet serene,
> That bayonet did in hate impale
> Along some disputed winding trail,
> That now endless seemed in burning sand,
> To captives here in caravan.

Finding themselves stationed on the Philippines in 1941, most American soldiers thought they had stumbled upon a dream world from which they had no desire to be awakened. Beautiful blue skies, balmy weather, lush tropical plant life and the friendly Philippine people made them feel they were in paradise. On December 8, 1941, reality in the guise of Japanese bombers and invasion put an end to this dream. As one soldier described it in verse:

They sent us to the Philippines.
We thought it a vacation
This visit to the land of dreams
Proved our complete ruination

Soon after we had landed here
The Japs came down to meet us
With planes and bombs and tanks and guns
They all came down to greet us

Our tanks were rolled from Stotsenburg
Down to Batangas Bay
From there we hit Lingayen Gulf
Then to Bataan to stay

We covered all withdrawals too
In the darkness of the night
No infantry for close support
Though we howled with all our might

The Agno River line was held
With thirty M-3 tanks
Five and twenty good, long miles
Along the river's bank

No other troops available
To help us through the night
Our weapons mighty useless
Not even could we sight

The tanks were always last to leave
The active scene of strife
Our orders late or none at all
This was our daily life

So here we sit, in old Bataan
Just waiting for our aid
We listen to the radio—tell
How much U.S. has made!

Americans were caught off guard by the Japanese air attacks on December 8, 1941. For most of them the news of Pearl Harbor had barely been assimilated. Incompetence and unpreparedness plagued the attempts at defense. One group of men found their machine guns useless due to a lack of belted ammunition. The base armorer explained to them that ammunition for the automatic weapons was belted only as it was needed for the rifle range. Antiquated fuses prevented the artillery units, belonging to the 200th Coast Artillery at Clark Field from making adequate use of their weapons as only one shell in six exploded when fired. In addition, the 200th C.A. was handicapped by the absence of the calibrating equipment for their guns which had been at the Ordinance Department for adjustment since the unit arrived in September. The worst disaster of all was the initial destruction of the military planes as they stood on the air fields before they could strike any blows against the enemy. Almost 90 percent of the planes at Clark Field, for example, were destroyed when the Japanese hit the air base at 12:35 p.m. Lined up on the runway awaiting General MacArthur's orders for an air strike on Formosa, the planes made a perfect target for the Japanese bombers.

The Japanese had no intention of allowing the Americans to recover from the unexpectedness of the attack. Bombs continued to fall on the city of Manila leaving it a blackened, smoking ruin. In addition, the Japanese began land attacks on December 10, with an amphibious landing of 5,000 men at Appari to the south of Luzon. Another 5,000 men were put ashore at Vigan, to the north, on December 12. More troops continued to land December 14. Eighty transports disembarked at Lingayen Gulf and 40 at Laman Bay.

Initially there was little contact with the Japanese troops. However, this soon changed as the Japanese began to advance on Manila. Again and again, the American and Filipino forces fell back from the furious Japanese onslaught. Hindering their success was antiquated equipment and the early destruction of

the planes that were to have provided air cover. Unless rein-
forcements arrived, the American and Filipino forces would be
forced to leave the field of battle to the victorious Japanese. On
December 23, 1941, MacArthur decided that the only plan of
action left open for them to follow was WPO-3, a planned withdrawal to the Bataan Peninsula where the troops could fight a
delaying battle until the United States sent help. According to
Wainwright, "It was a bitter pill to swallow, for W. Plan Orange
No. 3 meant the last ditch: The long ago planned desperation
withdrawal to Bataan."

When the order came to implement WPO-3, it assumed the
form of a nightmare for the skeletonized 200th C.A., whose duty
it was to supervise the planned retreat of three divisions over
great distances to Bataan. The withdrawals and deployments
necessary to move the approximately 28,000 men (25,000 still
untrained) an average distance of 150 miles to Bataan was an
ordeal never to be forgotten.

General Albert M. Jones's South Luzon Force had a more
critical problem of retreat as it had to swing around Manila Bay
and duck into Bataan through the back way. Unfortunately there
was only one road and it had to cross the Pampanga River by
means of the Calumpit bridge to reach San Fernando Pumpunya
and the homestretch of the escape route to Bataan. Realizing
the bridge was a serious weak spot, the Japanese made an all out
attempt to reach and destroy it before the South Luzon Force
crossed the river. To guard against this eventuality, the American
forces stationed the batteries of the 200th C.A. around the bridge
and sent the 500 men left of the 91st Division, plus a regiment
of the 71st Division, north of Baliua, to guard the bridge. Despite
a hard pushing attack by the Japanese December 31, 1941, these
men managed to hold the bridge until the last of the stragglers
followed by the batteries of the 200th C.A. crossed the river early
January 1, 1942. Within minutes of their arrival the bridge was
destroyed to prevent the pursuit of the Japanese.

The withdrawal, as Wainwright liked to think of the action,
was now complete. Occupying 200 square miles of the Bataan
Peninsula were over 100,000 people. Of this number, 78,000
were army troops who had almost no military training or experience. Approximately 15 percent of these were actually

Americans. Another 20,000 were Filipinos who had fled with the army rather than accept the friendship offered by their Japanese liberators. Also, there were some 6,000 civilian employees of the army. And scattered across this area were the few supplies and scanty equipment the beleaguered defenders had managed to bring with them. Artillery, tanks, and other vehicles, gasoline and oil stocks, and stores of ammunition and food. Command posts hospitals, communication centers, and other vital installations a fighting army needs were also dispersed across this terrain. As one American staff officer put it, "Bataan was so crowded that bombers could drop their pay loads at almost any point or place and hit something of military value."

On January 7, the North and South Luzon Forces were redesignated the I and II Philippine Corps. The I Philippine Corps under the leadership of General Wainwright defended the west section of Bataan while the II Philippine Corps led by General Parker guarded the eastern one. The Philippine Corps consisted of a motley band of fighting men. For example, the I Philippine Corps consisted of Brigadier General Fidel Brougher's 11th Division, Brigadier General Clinton Sequndo's 1st Division, Brigadier General Clinto Pierce's 71st Division, Brigadier General Luther R. Stevens' 91st Division, the 45th Infantry Regiment of the Philippine Scouts, the remnants of the 26th Cavalry under Col. Lee C. Vance, a small group of planeless fliers and ground crewmen, some air corps engineers, a detachment of 450 sailors, and the 2nd Philippine Constabulary. Also, it was mostly made up of Philippine nationals who had been inducted and mobilized anywhere from a few months to a few days before the War began. It was going to be a hard if not impossible task to mold this varied group into a cohesive fighting unit.

When MacArthur was ordered to leave the Philippines in March for Australia, Wainwright was appointed Commander of the Philippine Garrison. As a result Wainwright moved from Bataan to Corregidor leaving Major General Edward P. King in charge of the defense of Bataan. Within a few short weeks, King would surrender the forces under his care to prevent further needless bloodshed.

Besides this, the Bataan defenders found themselves having to deal with the problem of total unpreparedness for what was happening. While the American high command managed successfully to withdraw its troops to the Peninsula, the officers in charge neglected to transport adequate provisions for the men. In addition, the United States Government had provided the Philippine Command with weapons and ammunition dating back to WW I and with men who had little or no training. The raw Filipino soldiers who had been drafted shortly before the War had the habit of evacuating the front lines whenever a shot was fired or night fall descended. As a result, the American units many times would find themselves facing the enemy alone. Ammunition was a hit-or-miss affair. "There were five rounds to a clip and you would have two or three duds in each clip. When one round failed to fire you would eject it and try the next one." To James Gautier, according to R. Jackson Scott, hand grenades were virtually useless as only two out of the 25 his unit tried exploded. In fact, they could be downright dangerous as some exploded too soon and took an arm off the thrower. Another soldier complained about his WW I Enfield rifle. "Damn, I was innocent. I thought the army was supposed to give a guy something better than a flintlock to fight with." Fighting under such far from ideal circumstances created soldiers of tempered steel.

> Ask at Limay and Balanga
> Where the outpost burrowed like moles
> Where the sky-trained flying soldiers
> Died in Infantry holes.
>
> And last seek the silent jungles
> Where the unburied bodies lie
> Asleep by their rusting rifles
> The men who had learned how to die
>
> Who squeezed the Garanda trigger?
> Who met the tanks on a mare
> Who flew the primary trainers
> When "Zeroes" were in the air?
>
> Who watched the bombbays open
> Day after endless day
> Who stayed with the anti-aircraft
> With tons of H.E. on the way

Who, but your immature youngsters
The forgotten men of Bataan.

We were soft, we were weaklings and aimless
We believed in ourselves alone
But now we are tempered with fire
We are ready U.S.—to come home.

Another hardship facing the beleaguered troops was the critical food situation. Only a 30-day stock of unbalanced field rations for 100,000 people had been brought to Bataan. To make this last, MacArthur ordered half rations January 6, 1942. Theoretically this meant an American would receive 36 ounces of food each day and a Filipino 32 ounces. Unfortunately neither one ever received even 30 ounces after the end of January. Fresh meat was issued twice a week when it was available. Usually it was carabao (water buffalo). When these animals were gone, the 250 horses and 48 pack mules of the 26th Cavalry Regiment became the new meat source. By the middle of March, this supply was gone. One soldier described his fare: "Fish and rice twice a day. No coffee, no tea, no milk, no sugar, no nothing but fish and rice. We are completely out of everything." To supplement their diet, the Americans roamed the countryside. "We were eating lizards, monkeys, and anything else that came under our guns. The life expectancy of anything that walked, crawled, or flew on lower Bataan was practically nil." Eventually, the foraging activities were stopped by the exhaustion of the plant and animal life of Bataan. The peninsula had not been big or fertile enough to provide extra food for over 100,000 people. Forced now to rely solely on their army rations for sustenance, the troops found them insufficient. By March the ration provided 1,000 calories daily to men who were expending between 3,500 to 4,000 calories every day. As a result of this calorie deficit, the troops showed serious muscle waste and depletion of fat reserves. Beriberi, in its incipient stages, was universally rampant. Throughout the command, weakened by malnutrition, the soldiers found themselves vulnerable to even the most minor ailments. Weight loss averaged 22 lbs. The men suffered from diseases including malaria, dengue, scurvy, beriberi, and amoebic dysentery. Faced with all this, the men found themselves joking at their situation to make it bearable, as in these verses:

> When they git to talking medals,
> And the battle souvenir,
> Like the Silver Star and Purple Heart,
> And this here "Croy de Gear"—
>
> I ain't got no fancy ribbons
> So I feel a little queer;
> But they sure ought to be a medal
> For guys with diarrhea.
>
> My guts is shot all full o'holes,
> Like a bullet-drilled me clear,
> And blood! I've lost a bucketful
> From this here diarrhea.
>
> But after you lose your innards,
> There ain't nothing else to fear;
> And I bet God has got a medal,
> For guys with diarrhea.

The defenders needed something to keep their spirits up. The lack of medical supplies and proper medical treatment made the slightest wound a danger. By March, many of the casualties were developing gas gangrene. When this happened, the doctors had to cut open the skin to let the gas escape. While many patients survived, a number did not. Also, general health by now was so poor that many patients died when anesthesia was administered.

> How we fought in the heat, rain and stink,
> Only to be captured to starve and die.
> Months of jungle fighting
> Enemy bombers over our head
> Malaria mosquitoes biting
> Of the whistle and whine of lead
> Sleepless nites of waiting
> For the help that never came

Never so tense and grating,
Bleeding sore and lame
Prayers and fears for loved ones
Shed so far away from home
Tears for our buddies who bled and died
With cuts, bruises and mangled bones
Ten thousand miles away.

By the end of March, living conditions were unbearable. There was the perpetual choking dust and the hard ground that wracked the muscles of the emaciated soldiers. The terrific heat and scarcity of cigarettes made tempers flare. While the enemy planes overhead droned toward their targets, the continual buzzing of flies below drove everyone crazy. Artillery fire burst all around the men and the machine guns constantly buzzed and chattered. Occasionally there were the screams of a soldier who had been hit. Even at night enemy shells and flares lit up the jungle in a ghastly light as the monkeys' screaming mingled with the hooting of owls. To make matters even more unbearable, the men kept stumbling across the mutilated bodies of friends who had been captured by the Japanese. It looked as if the Japanese didn't take prisoners.

Eventually, the end came. It had only been a matter of time before the disease-ridden, exhausted, starving soldiers found they could fight no more. Early in April the Japanese began attacking in never-ending waves. The sick, weary men of Bataan stood no chance against these fresh troops. Again and again they fell back. General King, who had assumed command in March when Wainwright left Bataan to replace the departing MacArthur, decided the only way to save his men was to surrender. On April 9, 1942, King unconditionally surrendered the defenders of Bataan to Lieutenant General Masahare Homma.

The surrender was a bitter pill for the Americans to swallow. As one soldier put it, "We were the first troops in American history to surrender. I am sure this thought has remained with us to this day." In addition, there was some resentment about the help that never had come. Feelings of abandonment and disgrace flashed through heads.

You all know the grim story
—But there are those who didn't see,
The fall and disgrace of Old Glory,
—And what it meant to me.
Probably now we're forgotten
—By those who sent us to die,
To an unprepared island begotten
—By Dewey so noble and shy
Our country you know has billions
—In food, silver and gold
Personnel and material in trillions
—Why buddie! the half can't be told
Yes! We know she'll not be beaten
—Proud and true she'll always stand
And altho' our pride we have eaten
—On her shores we long to land.
But I wonder what our folks will think
—When we tell of this old "Bahay"
And how we fought in the heat, rain, and stink
—Only to be captured to starve and die
Months of jungle fighting
—Enemy bombers o'er our head
Malaria mosquitos biting
—Of the whistle and whine of lead
Sleepless nites of waiting
—For the help that never came
Never so tense and grating,
—Bleeding, sore and lame
Prayers and fears for loved ones
—Shed so far away from home
Tears for our buddies who bled and died
—With cuts, bruises and mangled bones
Dreaming of home and loved ones
—Ten thousand miles away
Listening to the roar of the big guns
—And its "Photo Joe" at the break of day
Does anyone call you a coward
—Because you broke and ran

When at last we were overpowered,
—And surrendered Corregidor and Bataan
They may think that's where it ended
—And from there out it was fun
But when in prison we were taken
—We found the fight had just begun
Thrown into mud bound prison camp
—To live with the rat, flea and lice
To suffer and die from disease or cramps
—From eating weeds and wormy rice
What happened to that Starry Flag
—O'er the Islands where it had flown
In its place a Jap sleeping bag
—And every nite on the grounds its thrown
They replaced her with the Flaming Wheel
—The symbol of Imperial Japan
But they can't replace the love we feel
—For Old Glory, Corregidor, and Bataan
The Good "Lord" we know is with you
—Hang not your head in shame
But lift your voice in prayer (yes do)
—For the help that never came.

Remembering the mutilated bodies of friends who had fallen into enemy hands, the disheartened soldiers wondered what their own fate would be under the enemy's power. Rumors that the Japanese were taking no prisoners passed up and down through the units. Added to this, there were emotional outbursts as the men burned the American flag to keep it from falling to the enemy. All the army equipment except personal items were destroyed. Word began to filter back to get rid of any Japanese souvenirs. Gradually, the men began to pull things back together. Some soldiers decided to head for the nearest road to await the Japanese, others decided to march to Mariuales.

When the defeated men finally met up with the Japanese, the soldiers found the situation worse than their most frightening nightmare. The Japanese accepted each surrender on an individual basis and were totally unpredictable about it. "They might give you a cigarette one minute and put a bayonet through you the next." According to Charles Baum, the first Japanese tanks he saw drew up beside some Filipinos ahead of the Americans. Without warning, the tanks opened fire and massacred every soldier. Then the tanks resumed their advance toward the Americans who were holding their breath as to their fate. Fortunately, the Japanese sergeant leading the tanks motioned his men past the prisoners. Besides being subjected to entirely random procedures, the defeated men found themselves threatened by acts of revenge. All the officers and noncommissioned officers of the 91st Division of the Philippine Army, about 350 to 400 men altogether, were ordered slain by a man believed to be General Altira Mara, 65th Brigade Commander, because many of his troops had died fighting the 91st. The men had their wrists tied behind their backs. Then from one side the Japanese officers started beheading the captives while the enlisted men bayoneted them in the back on the other. For over 2 hours this murder went on. The captives were beginning to realize, as one expressed it:

> When at last we were overpowered,
> —And surrendered Corregidor and Bataan
> They may think that's where it ended
> —And from there out it was fun
> But when in prison we were taken
> —We found the fight had just begun

The fight had just begun for these men. The Japanese wanted the captives evacuated from Bataan so they could launch a full-scale attack against Corregidor. As a result, the Japanese began moving the men to a detention camp in Central Luzon. This evacuation earned itself the name "The Bataan Death March." Most of the Americans and Filipinos were in bad health and in no condition for a long, hard march in their weakened condition. They were down to about a third of their normal weight. And almost all of them suffered from malaria, beriberi, malnutrition (no food for 3 or 4 days) and dysentery. But the malarial fevers described below tended to make the journey easier.

My sweetheart is Malaria,
And I met her in Bataan.
I'm just one of her many loves,
But still her favorite man.

Our love began with a tropic moon,
Where the river meets the sea;
And she spends her charms in other
    arms,
But always returns to me.
Our love is like all other loves,
She leaves me now and then;
But my fever burns and my love returns,
To embrace me once again.

In my lover's arms I tremble,
With hot and fevered brow;
But she holds me less in each fond caress,
So she'll be leaving now.

My sweetheart is Malaria,
And I met her in Bataan;
I'm just one love of her many loves,
But still her favorite man.

To make matters worse, an Army order came out of Manila stating "... any American captive who is unable to continue marching all the way to the concentration camp should be put to death in an area 200 meters off the highway." As a result, the Japanese had no mercy for stragglers. Anyone who fell was quickly bayoneted and left to die along the roadside. Others were just pulled off without rhyme or reason.

At Mariveles, where the river ran,
There joined that forlorn, tatter'd band
A bearded stranger, his eyes despair,
Whom I had seen, but God knows where
Ill and starving this wretched man,
To join captives here in caravan.

A bridge was crossed in that torrid Hell,
And they struck him there, but as he fell
His arms outstretched, and he clutched the rail;
Oh, God, his eyes, and so deathly pale,
As bleeding there, he tried to stand,
This captive fell from caravan.

This bearded wretch then for water cried,
A glistening bayonet pierced his side!
I turned my head from the bloody scene,
But looked back once more on his face serene,
Where dead he lay in the scorching sand,
This captive slain in caravan.

Out of the night with haunting wail,
Her song in grief, some nightingale
Sang in Balanga, battered town,
Now silent, but for this eerie sound;
Where blackened ruins held empty hand,
For captives starved in caravan.

Some shell-torn church in shadowed night,
Beside whose walls to await the light
Of the tropic dawn of another day,
Men laid down their packs, to sleep or pray;
Now starved and thirsting, weary band,
These captives here in caravan.

In the moonlight on that haunted scene,
I wept for the stranger, gaunt and lean,
And within the church to mourn our loss,
I beheld the stranger on the Cross!
There, my bearded stranger of Bataan,
The captive slain in caravan.

Sing once more the nightingales,
Their songs now lovely on moonlit trails;
And years pass on, but each night it seems
I return to Bataan in torturing dreams,

> Where this Stranger smiles and takes my hand,
> As I march captive there in caravan.

In addition to the senseless killing, other hardships faced by the exhausted soldiers on the march was the lack of food and water, the dearth of rest stops, the intense heat, and the refusal of the Japanese of even comfort stops.

Distance varied according to where Bataan men joined the march, length varied as to whether they stayed and the length of stay in rest stops; food and water varied.

> Now I've seen a heap of water
> In some places that I've been;
> In lots of lakes and oceans
> That I've done some fishing in;
> And I've seen some rains and cloudbursts
> Where a lot of water ran,
> But I never knowed the stuff was precious
> Till the Death March from Bataan.
>
> I was captured at Cabcaben,
> My canteen was nearly dry;
> Them Nips pushed me in the road,
> With the others dragging by.
> "Twenty dollars for a swallow,
> Jest a little in my hand!"
> That's what they thought of water
> On the Death March from Bataan.
>
> The road was hot and scorching
> As the henges off of Hell,
> And before we reached Balanga,
> There was lots of men that fell.
> But I kept on that road a-stumbling,
> With my throat all full of sand,
> And I never knowed what water was
> On the Death March from Bataan.
>
> Jest this side of San Fernando,
> I seen a waterhole

That dead men was a-floating in,
Where carabao had rolled,
So I jumped in head first,
And scooped water with my hand,
But that's the best drink I ever had
On the Death March from Bataan.

Well I've drank a lot of water
Since them days on old Bataan,
And now I drink it by the bucket,
But I'm still a thirsty man
So sometimes I set and figure,
That when my soldiering days are done,
I'm going to buy myself a river,
And jest set and watch it run.

On the way to Balanga, the prisoners found their situation deteriorated rapidly.

Before we had gone two miles our shirts were stripped from our bodies. The sun reached straight above us, beating down on our bare heads. My head began to ache in the blistering heat. My eyes seemed to bulge from my head. I wanted water more than anything. We kept walking and the heat seemed to search out all the strength in me.

Soon the hot sun had burned and irritated the captives' skin, and dehydrated them: "The skin on our noses was peeling, our mouths became raw and sore, the skin began to crack and I was unable to spit as there just was no saliva there." The craving for water became almost intolerable. Yet, if anyone attempted to satisfy his desire, he risked his life. The Japanese shot or bayoneted anybody who tried to fill his canteen with water or attempted to steal a drink from muddy carabao holes. Still some men tried it, willing to pay the price as long as they could taste the coolness of water again. Besides the Japanese were poor shots, so there was a chance one could get away with it. Staying on the inside ranks of the column, the thirsty men found they had a better chance of succeeding in obtaining drinks from muddy contam-

inated carabao wallow that sometimes had dead swollen bodies
in them:

> Whenever we would come upon a pool of water, I'd
> fall down face first into it. Then I'd drink as much as I
> could as fast as I could before getting up again. One day,
> however, I got a nice big surprise. About four feet away
> from me was a big body all puffed up and bloated. At first
> I hadn't seen it, so I already had consumed some water. It
> was really good water.

Occasionally, a Japanese guard would give the prisoners
permission to drink from these holes. At times the cocky captors
would use the defeated men's thirst to torture them. One group
came to a cool mountain stream in the hot afternoon sun. Waiting
for authorization to drink, the parched men licked their dry,
cracked lips. Suddenly one of them could stand it no more, so
he rushed to the water and put his face into it. A guard went
over to the kneeling man, raised his sword high, and then
brought it down on the bent neck. The head rolled away staining
the water a violent red. The body, stationary for a moment, suddenly gushed blood and fell into the stream. Yelling, the guards
ordered the men back onto the road. They never tasted the cool,
delicious water of the stream that had cost a man his life.

Besides the harshness of the sun and the tormenting thirst
it caused, the constant presence of death made the march an
ordeal. Within a few hours of starting the trek the captured men
began to pass the dead and the dying; soon they grew used to
it:

> I passed a man lying in the road with his head smashed
> in, and then another, writhing in misery, clutching his belly
> in bloody hands. A bayonet had been driven through his
> intestines. Soon it became commonplace and I saw scores
> and finally hundreds like them. I began to think only of
> lifting my feet one at a time and putting them down.

The Japanese were following the order from Manila which
called for those who failed to keep up, to be put to death. Reaching the end of their endurance, prisoners dropped out of the

columns to meet their death. In the beginning, it was just a few, but the number soon mounted as the hungry, disease-ridden men found the last of their strength gone. Those suffering from malaria were especially affected by the march since the hot sun was hard on their fever-and-chill-racked bodies. At first the defeated men did not realize what was happening to the sick and exhausted men that fell beside the road. They believed the rumors that the injured and the sick were being picked up by trucks which would carry them to where they could get medical aid. Joseph D. Lajzer tells of how he learned the truth:

> So I as a twenty-year-kid I said to myself why should I walk and walk and walk. When I can get a ride on a truck. So I slack back until I was about 30–40 yards from the end of my company. And I acted like I was crippled using a sugar cane for a walking cane. When I came to this wooded bridge—alone, my company in front of me. And a Jap guard on the other side—I say on my left side, and about 15 yards away from me. When he bent down like a football player, his gun and bayonet looking at me and he started to run at me his bayonet looking right at me when I made my move. I move so fast that I was in front of my company in two shakes. Tell all the G.I.'s on the march that the Japs were picking up the crippled and sick on a bayonet instead of a truck.

Once the prisoners realized what was happening to their comrades they left behind, they tried to help the injured and ill men stay up with the group. According to Louis B. Read, "If a guy was stumbling and acting like he was going to fall, you would grab him on either side and try to hold him up and march him till the column stopped. Unfortunately, it was not always possible to do this, since those who helped were not in much better shape than the ones who had reached the end of their endurance. What happened then was that the weakened men were passed back in the ranks until no one could hold them any longer, and they fell out. In the beginning, the guards watching the last group of the marching columns, had finished the stragglers off. Eventually, they ignored those who fell. The captured men at the back of the column were wondering why the Japanese had changed policies when they heard shots behind them. Then they knew a clean-up squad of Japanese was following them. And the pistol cracks acted as a goad to the weary men: "Oh, God, I've got to keep going. I can't stop. I can't die like that." Surrounded by death, the marching men lived with the expectation they could be the next to die.

> They said we were soft, we were aimless
> They said we were spoiled past reclaim
> We had lost the American Spirit
> We were blots on America's name.
>
> We were useless weaklings and drifters
> And the last youth census reveals
> We had lost the faith of our fathers
> We had sacrificed muscles for wheels.
>
> The old men wept for their country
> And sighed for the days of yore
> And, somehow we half believed them
> But that was before the War.
>
> Before we heard the bomb shriek
> And the howling, ugly and shrill
> That ripples across the rice field
> When the Nippy comes in for the kill.
>
> Before we had lived on hunger
> And rumors and nerve and pain
> Before we had seen our buddies
> Dying among the cane.
>
> Our War! our own little rat trap
> The hopeless defense of Bataan
> An advance guard, yet no main body
> Yet a thorn in the side of Japan.
>
> So now we can laugh at our Elders
> And now we can give them the lie

We held that line that couldn't be held
When they struck at Abucay.

Soft? and Weaklings? and Shameless?
Go where the steel was sowed
And ask of the Endless Fox-Graves
That dot the Hacienda Road.

For those who survived this march to the concentration
camp, one soldier summed up their lives:

In a camp of bamboo barracks
Way deep in the Philippines
Are a group of forgotten warriors
With nothing left but dreams.

They are fighting a greater battle
Than the one they fought and lost.
It's a battle against the elements
A battle with life the cost.

Some come thru that awful torture
Like the days and nites in hell,
In that weary struggle for Bataan
Where many brave men fell.

Now it's not how much you know
Nor how quick you hit the ditch
It's not the eating you once held
On whether you're poor or rich.

No one cares who you knew back
  home
Nor what kind of life you led,
It's just how long you can stick it out—
That governs your life, instead—

Now the battles they're fighting
Are with mosquitos and disease,

> But with better living conditions,
> They'll win their fight with ease—
>
> It's rice for breakfast noon and night
> It rains most every day
> They sleep on bamboo stalks at nite
> They've no better place to lay.
>
> They eat from old tin cans
> That they are lucky enough to get,
> And the medics they should have
> They haven't seen us yet.

The arrival in camp after an ordeal that no one should have had to experience may have been a relief. It also brought up the question: What are they going to do to us now?

It was during the long wait for help to come that the poetry was written. Each of the men having something in his mind that he was using "poetic relief" in an attempt to expel events of the death march from his troubled mind. Most of the poetry differed only in the events that were set to prose. However, the poem, *The Fall of Old Glory*, seemed to try to defend defeat—a defeat that needed no defending. They were sent to fight a war with little or no training, and without weapons to defend themselves. Only one poem had a mention of "loved ones" back home; strangely, there were no others about their "loved ones"—no mention of wives or family—though there might have been, and these poems were too personal to share.

I feel sure there were times when most of the men, during Filipino sunset, turned their eyes toward home with their head turned slightly upward. It could have very well been one of these men that first used the words that are now in a very beautiful song:

> Well, I can dream can't I?

BIBLIOGRAPHY

Babler, E. J. 1220 days in Hell. Private papers, Waupun, Wisconsin.

Brown, C. *Bars from Bilibad Prison*, San Antonio, Texas: Naylor Co., 1947.

Considine, R. (Ed.). *General Wainwright's story*. Garden City, New York; Doubleday & Company, Inc., 1946.

Dyess, W. E. *The Dyess story: The eye-witness account of the death march*. New York; G. P. Putnam's Sons, 1944.

Hawes, M. D. Diary. El Paso, Texas.

Miller, E. B. *Bataan uncensored*. Long Prairie, Minnesota; The Hart Publications, 1949.

Oral History Collection. North Texas State University, Denton, Texas, Vol. 91, Vol. 138.

Chapter 13

POETRY AND THE BODY POLITIC

Charles Taylor

I want to bring back a forgotten metaphor which I ran across in Sir John Davies' *Nosce Teipsum,* the first philosophical poem in the English language, published in 1599.

The metaphor Davies used is 'the body politic.' It requires us to transcend our current tradition of scientific reductionism which finds truth in the smallest entity—an atom, or an individual—and instead to see the whole society, the whole community, as one body—the body politic. We are one: one earth, one people. Our words strain at a concept which is perhaps more easily intuited than logically understood—animus mundi, the collective unconscious—body politic.

Of course, it is a paradox. We are many, we are legion, as well as being one. But the individuality in our culture is constantly stressed. The other side is harder to grasp. It is harder to recognize that our skin does not end at the skin, that we are connected. Our brains and nervous systems flash messages, whether or not we actually speak to one another. Often an idea or a spirit will be "in the air" and we all consciously or unconsciously participate in that spirit: We all participated in the guilt and rage of the Vietnam War, whatever our politics; in the 1590s, when

John Davies lived, people felt a sense of despair, the end of the century blues.

It is possible to imagine that everyone in an audience is all one body, that the citizens in a city are all one body. The myths tell us we all came from the same parents. In Judeo-Christian terms it's Adam and Eve. In biological terms, it is one species, Homo sapiens.

If we accept the metaphor that we are a body politic, different leaves on one great tree—a very physical metaphor appealing for its materiality—then we might grant that the body politic experiences *illnesses:* illnesses both physical and psychological. The high rates of cancer, ulcers, and heart disease in the United States are signals from the body politic that there are problems in the body politic. The herpes and AIDS epidemics are further signals that something is wrong. We as poets or poetry therapists must avoid the tendency to see these illnesses solely as those of the suffering individuals. We like to shuffle the sick off to hospitals or clinics and pretend they are not a part of us, just as we like to pack the aged off to retirement homes and the war-wounded to veterans hospitals. As a group we like the image of clean and healthy and strong. We don't like to admit weaknesses. Yet it is the human condition for bodies to be weak at times, and for the body politic to have weaknesses. One of the healing functions of poetry—in the face of society's attempts to deny its humanity, its weaknesses, and mortality by sweeping the sick and infirm out of sight—is to remind us of our darkness and our weakness, our human imperfectness, and to accept imperfection as part of what defines us as human and different from machines.

I used to wonder, when focusing on poetry as a healing art, where did negative or angry or depressed poetry fit in. Such poetry, I used to think, was not life-affirming and healthy. Now I see that a truly "healthy" attitude accepts to a certain degree the humanity of disease, of weakness. I am not saying we should not try to cure people; but rather that we should not hate disease as the devil.

Sometimes the psychiatric movement gets too focused on solving an individual's problems. Such a focus has a certain practicality. It is easier to heal one person than to heal the entire body politic. Some illnesses at this point in time cannot be healed and must be accepted. But when healing is a *possibility*, as we hope it is with cancer or herpes or AIDS, then perhaps an approach in terms of the body politic is necessary, for if the communal body is sick, we cannot be well. We are not separate. When the bell tolls, "send not to know for whom the bell tolls; it tolls for thee."

How does the poet see his audience? Does he imagine a single person sitting alone in a room reading a book? If so, and if the poet is interested in poetry as a healing art, then his approach, like that of most psychologists, will be more individualistic. But suppose the poet gives readings and is used to an audience response, a collective response to his work. Then the poet's approach, as a practicioner of an oral medium that goes back to ancient times, will be less privatized, more communally oriented. The audience is a large chunk right there before him of the body politic.

The poet in speaking to this audience may offer emotional catharsis in the old Aristotelian sense; but our healing practices can involve more than this. We may seek to *name* emotions felt collectively by a group. At present, the body politic suffers under the stress of changing relationships between men and women. Poets can name for an audience their emotional pain and to some extent free that audience. However, the poet's healing function goes beyond this. The poet speaks of values and ethics and visions. He suggests where the body politic errs in its collective behavior, perhaps through satirical poetry, and suggests a more human, healing behavior.

If we view society as a living organism rather than as a mechanical structure to be repaired through reform, or completely destroyed and rebuilt by revolution, we gain many insights into poetry's function. If we say the poet is a healer who speaks to the body politic—sometimes curing, sometimes soothing, sometimes criticizing, sometimes celebrating the tragic imperfections—is that language not useful? The poet can be a prophet like Cassandra in the story of Troy. Cassandra, condemned by the gods to be ignored, found her counsels and warnings rejected. This seems the image of the artist as social prophet. Look at what happened to Ezra Pound. He ended up a traitor and a crazy, confined to a mental hospital.

But if we change our language perhaps we can reach a new outlook: the poet as healer of the body politic—that delivers us from the onus of certain political assumptions. The poet is not the only healer of the body politic, of course; many artists and nonartists participate in the grand healing, which goes on all the time. And the poet will do other things to heal besides write poetry. Maria Sabrina in Mexico chanted poems, but she used other methods of treatment.

The Chinese medical tradition has a metaphor for a man with a tumor. In one drawing they picture a man with a bump on his head. In the next picture the bump is gone and a bird is depicted flying away. This is so different from the Western metaphor of killing germs or cutting the evil thing out and destroying it. Suppose that poets saw themselves as releasing from the body politic, through their words, birds trapped where they do not belong? You laugh. Good. But I am serious. I think of Norman Cousin's laugh therapy for cancer. Why do poets not write more laughter into their poems, good hearty laughter, something like the Archie Bunker show which during the Vietnam era did much to relieve tension and anger in the American body politic? Norman Mailer called the writings of Saul Bellow "cancerous"—meaning Mailer did not believe the sorrow and resignation found in some of Bellow's work was healthy for the body politic of readers.

If we could alter our language, our perceptions of what we do could improve. Some poetry has condescendingly been called "protest poetry." That is a negative term, used by those who like quiet to tune down those who speak up. Instead, such poetry could be called poetry therapy for the body politic.

The body politic is a complex and sensitive yet highly adaptive and strong organism. Usually it does not require heroic measures. Often a small thing will be the key to finding balance, restoring health. The number of poets is small. We feel like useless Cassandras. But the healing of the body politic may not require many, since the body strongly desires to heal itself. The number needed for healing may be far less than a numerical majority.

Chapter 14

PRISON POETRY

Gene Burd

Prisons produce and put to use poetry for therapeutic purposes. From the depths of Dante's punishment in purgatory to *Cool Hand Luke* 600 years later in the sixties, the poems of imprisonment have been created under the chains of constraint and confinement. They have expressed the state and sentiments of the prisoner, and have helped him endure isolation and incarceration as well as hope for release and reformation.

Both the image and reality of prison have generated poetry. One of England's great Romantic poets, Richard Lovelace, himself jailed during the civil war of the 1600s, wrote in Gatehouse Prison his ode *To Althea* proclaiming that "Stone walls do not a prison make, Nor iron bars a cage . . ." Oscar Wilde's more pessimistic message from prison pronounced that "The vilest deeds, like poison weeds, / Thrive well in prison air. It is only what is good in men, / That wastes and withers there."[1]

Poetry is abundant in the many prison newspapers in the U.S. and provides a creative and therapeutic outlet for self-expression. America's first penal newspaper, *Forlorn Hope,* founded March 24, 1800 in New York State Prison, published a long poem bemoaning the imprisonment of war veterans for

debt stemming from war service.[2] Through the years, prisoners
writing poetry have filled such newspapers with their verses of
dreams and disappointment, fears and failures, love and lust,
women and war, food and force, sex and sadness, hate and harm,
authority and anarchy, memories and mourning of home and
family, letters and laments on culture and conscience, and the
eternal analogy of prison to the frustrations of life itself—both
inside and outside the walls.[3]

The prison community is a microcosm of many of the outside
"minority communities" which are often similarly segregated,
isolated, contained, or restricted by reason of a different social,
economic, political or religious life-style; for reasons of race or
ethnicity, age or physical handicaps. For them also, poetry is a
means to communicate freely what often cannot be said through
established outlets. Less restrictive than prose, poetry breaks
down barriers, as poets cry out in rage or praise. For them, poetry
is often cheaper than psychiatry, and probably at times more
effective.[4]

Since what goes on inside prisons often remains unexamined
and unreported to the outside,[5] the general public presumably
concerned about the effectiveness of prisons often must depend
on mass media coverage of prison riots, or on the revelations of
prison poets, whose "light from another country" tells how prisoners use poetry to develop self-awareness and adapt to cruelty
and brutality.[6]

The more distant past has also been revealed by poets. A
Sing Sing inmate in 1878–1888, J.T. Connors, wrote more than
100 poems, songs, and anecdotes on topics ranging from love
of mother and Ireland to a "Hash Song" reviewing jailhouse cui-
sine of "bad beef and 'taters'."[7]

Sexual conditions in prisons have been both expressed and
endured by poems which "reveal the bitterness of denial and
frustration, the throbbing, ever present ache for sex fulfillment."
Such poems "afford an insight into the emotional life of prisoners
. . . reveal the stark vividness of their suppressed sexual life and
desires which are sublimated into verses . . . often echoing noble
desires, seeking to capture beautiful images and responding to
the urge to creative writing, regardless how crude the result may
be. . ."[8] To make a more normal sexual adjustment in prison,

"Inmates will memorize vulgar poems and doggerel" as a substitute for sexual experience.[9]

Poetic sublimation for such basic urges as sex and food may
have been more common 50 years ago before more recent freedom in both literature and social demands both inside and out
of prison. Some inside the prisons feel that too much censorship
on sexual literature may hinder correction and rehabilitation and
be self-defeating.[10] Poetry therapy has been used to treat
prisoners[11] and drug addicts,[12] and suggested as a supplement
to prisoners' experiences, such as gardening.[13] The longtime de-
bate on the therapeutic value of prisons is being revitalized by
the potential for use of an ancient method of emotional and
spiritual healing in the form of poetry. One reflection is that
"the current dilemma facing correctional agents reminds one of
the healer who sets out to 'cure' a population afflicted by some
age-old disease."[14]

Prison poetry can also become a political and social therapy
as confinement has led to literary introspection about ideas often
contrary to the established system which incarcerated those
thinkers and their thoughts. All those who have been jailed for
political or ideological deviance have not been poets or poetic,
nor have all been equally admired, but their poetic and prison
vision overlap in the literary tradition: Socrates, Paul, Galileo,
Columbus, Thomas More, Defoe, John Bunyan, Dostoyevski,
O'Henry, Hitler, Eugene Debs, Herman Melville, Jack London.
The myth of great men imprisoned is an inspirational theme in
the prison press.[15] Whether imprisoned in the Confederate
South, Soviet Siberia, South Vietnam, South America, Attica or
Alcatraz, prison writings are rich with poetic images of the crim-
inal and artist as a victim.[16]

Blacks have written volumes of poetry in prison along with
the literature of Malcolm X's *Autobiography*, Eldridge Cleaver's
Soul on Ice, and George Jackson's *Soledad Brother*.[17] Beyond
American civil conflict at home in the 1960s, the Vietnam War
abroad generated poetry on both sides, from the prison poems
of Ho-Chi-Minh,[18] to the poetry of the Berrigan brothers op-
posing the war. For Daniel Berrigan, "writing was as integral to
his life in prison as counseling, or rapping, or organizing, or
listening to the anguish of a prison brother." His prison poems
were "born of the grief and glory of prison life, (and) are door-

ways to a great spirit." In his 19 months of lockup, "he maintained a vision, a vision of nonviolent resistance, a vision of community formation."[19]

Poetry also served as therapy for American prisoners of war whose "bodies were imprisoned, but their minds sought freedom . . . through verse, as the poet POWs of the Hanoi Hilton."[20] They wrote of missed love, of their homeland, of prison rodents in sincere and often eloquent phrases. One Commander, James Hutton of Lakeland, Florida, wrote a poem *To America's Children*, telling them that "If you had been locked in a room, / All alone for many a month on end, / Then you would know how a rat or a mouse, / Could become a prisoner's friend."[21]

Both military, social and political imprisonment can ignite the poetic fires. Poet George Wither (1588-1667) was jailed for his satire on society, and like Leigh Hunt, wrote poems from his cell. So has Sara Jane Moore, who tried to kill President Ford.[22] The prison writings of Latin American guerrilla Regis Debray once poured from his cell in Bolivia,[23] and the prison poems of Russian poet Yuli Markovich Daniel (as he was grilled by the Soviet KGB) revealed "his despair and longing for those he loves, his loyalty to his friends and fears that his loyalty to his country might be doubted, (and) his sarcastic contempt for his jailers."[24] Thus he wrote: "There is no way for me to dodge this trouble/ The whip will find me everywhere/ And yet the white towel of cowardice/ Will not be thrown into the ring."[25]

In addition to poetry as prison therapy and political manifesto, poems can become types of legal documents. A poem on freedom and escape by drug cultist Timothy Leary was found in his prison locker room after he escaped and was read as evidence in court.[26] A Canadian, Jack McCann, serving 18 years for armed robbery, set himself afire in frustration over 754 days of solitary confinement. Dr. Stephen Fox told the court such punishment was "a serious undermining of the capacity to feel and communicate," and one of McCann's poems was read in court as evidence of his experience as *My Home is Hell.* The first and last verses indicating sophistication of techniques shown in the use of internal rhyme, are as follows:[27]

> My home is hell in one small cell
> That no man wants to own.

> For here I spend my life
>   condemned
> A man the world disowns.
>
> ....
> To those who steal the things I feel,
> And sow my heart with sorrow,
> Each farewell I bid in hell
> Is lost in each tomorrow.

Poetry helps prisoners break down barriers between themselves and others and with the outside world. Journalists like H.L. Mencken and Erle Stanley Gardner were receptive to the writings of prisoners. Poetry anthologies of prisoners' work are becoming more common. The poetry of Joseph John Maloney from the Missouri State Penitentiary appeared in literary little magazines, the *Christian Science Monitor,* and the *Kansas City Star,* which called it "some of the most powerful ever to come out of Mid-America". The *Star's* book editor wrote that Maloney's poems "can hit you like a fist, then dim your sight" with their honest, "muscular manner.".[28]

Prison poetry is in the writing tradition of participant/observer journalism. The writers write from their own experience. They are the best equipped to provide this therapeutic catharsis. In doing so, they create a sense of prison community and commonality, gain greater power over their own emotional lives, and become less dependent on the outside world for their self-confidence and self-control. Gardner believed that prison writing developed insight into life and character, and developed the writer's sympathetic perception as well as his skills.[29]

Prison administrators have found that creative self-expression by prisoners brings not only a sense of accomplishment, but helps them understand their own behavior better. One prisoner at Huntsville Prison in Texas 20 years ago decided to write poetry after reading a poem which inspired him. In describing his poetry-writing, he said "I pull an emotion out of someplace deep down inside me, and when I do I feel as though I'd ripped a chain off my soul."[30]

Prisoners on death row have been known to take a more positive attitude toward a short life as a result of their writing—

including poetry. William Witherspoon, a death row prisoner in the Cook County jail in Chicago, taught prisoners how to write as therapy, and used a poetic description of their transformation: "A rose comes to its fullest bloom when it is plucked . . . and put in a vase to die."[31] Psychologists have found that poetry is a useful therapeutic tool in helping prisoners to deal with their problems,[32] and prison poetry has found expression through radio,[33] as well as print, and also in poetic form in theatrical drama.[34] Inside and outside prisons, therapists may want to explore poetry.[35]

The artistic[36] and poetic urge can help prisoners survive and create at the same time. What better method to heal the wounds of mind and soul, to open windows instead of close doors, to break down walls instead of building them, and to unlock life itself from the hobbles and handcuffs used by the guards in the garrison, whose "Stone walls do not a prison make. . . ."?

REFERENCES

1. Nelson, V. F. *Prison days and nights.* New York: Garden City Publishing Co., 1932, p. 147.

2. Baird, R. N. Prison publications as a creative outlet for self-expression, pp. 98–111; Selected writings, pp. 115–156; Directory of publications, pp. 176–198. In *The penal press.* Evanston, IL: Northwestern University, 1967.

3. Famous prison newspapers include Stillwater, Minnesota, *Prison Mirror,* 1887; Sing Sing *Star of Hope,* 1899; Leavenworth, Kansas, *New Era,* 1914; The Illinois *Menard Time,* 1934; Huntsville, Texas, *Echo,* 1924; San Quentin *News,* 1940; Washington, D.C., *Time and Tied,* 1946; Folson, California, *Observer,* 1947.

4. Burd, G. Magazines and the minority messages of blacks and poets. Paper for Association for Education in Journalism, Berkeley, California, August 1969; Poetry as communication: Its relevance to revolt, politics and protest. Remarks to Patrick Henry High School, Minneapolis, Minnesota, June 21, 1970.

5. vanden Heuvel, W. J. The press and the prisons. *Columbia Journalism Review,* May/June 1972, pp. 35–40.

6. Bruchac, J. (Ed.). The light from another country: Poetry from American prisons, *Greenfield Review*, 1984.

7. Weiss, D. Songs from the yard: Sing Sing's lost poet. *American Heritage*, October 1979, *30*, 18–21.

8. Fishman, J. F. Prison poetry, Appendix A. In *Sex in prison*. New York: National Literary Press, 1934, pp. 217–238.

9. Clemmer, D. *The prison community* New York: Rinehart, 1958, p. 259.

10. Chang, D. H. & Armstrong, W. B. (Eds.). *The prison—Voices from the inside*. Cambridge: Schenkman, 1972.

11. Feeling poor lately? Try a few doses of poetry—"Poem therapy", the latest thing. Denver *Post*, August 14, 1972, p. 14.

12. Pauley, G. Poetry: New therapy for drug addicts. *Houston Post*, October 1, 1972, p. 6CC.

13. Tripp, N. Prison, potatoes and poetry. In Vermont inmates are raising vegetables and their self-esteem. *Horticulture*, October 1980, *58*, pp. 24ff.

14. Hazelrigg, L. E. (Ed.). *Prison within society—A reader in penology*. Garden City, NY: Doubleday, 1968, p. 269.

15. Baird, p. 99.

16. Franklin, H. B. *Victim as criminal and artist—Literature from the American prison*. New York: Oxford University Press, 1978; Debs, E. *Walls and bars*. Chicago: Socialist Party, 1927.

17. Prison poetry. *Essence*, April 1973, *3*, 50.

18. Ho-Chi-Minh. From prison diary: Poems. *The Nation*, May 6, 1968, *206*, 606.

19. Berrigan, D. *Prison poems* (Foreword by P. Berrigan). Greensboro, NC: Unicorn Press, 1973, p. 75.

20. Associated Press. PW ordeal reflected in poetry. Austin *American*, March 30, 1973.

21. *Ibid.*

22. Debray, R. *Prison writings* New York: Random House, 1970.

23. Bachmann, M. A cell of one's own (Includes poetry of Sara Jane Moore). *San Francisco Magazine*, May 1983, *25*, 25.

24. Daniel, Y. M. *Prison poems* (D. Burg & A. Boyars, trans.). London: Calder and Boyars, 1971, p. 14.

25. *Ibid*, p. 61.

26. Associated Press. Leary poem ruled usable as evidence. Austin *American*, March 17, 1973.

27. Jackson, M. *Prisoners of isolation: Solitary confinement in Canada*. Toronto: Toronto, 1983, p. 69–71.

28. Campbell, J. Thanksgiving: What have I to be thankful for. *The Echo*, November 1964, p. 1.

29. Gardner, E. S. The importance of the prison press. Nevada State Penitentiary *Sagebrush*, February 1958.

30. Menn, T. Books of the day. *Kansas City Star*, September 3, 1967, p. 8D.

31. Nolte, R. Prisoners learning to write in death row of county jail. *Chicago Tribune*, April 17, 1966, p. 6, Section 1.

32. Wright Williams, Ph.D., staff psychologist, Veteran's Hospital, Houston, Texas, who has worked with prisoners in West Virginia.

33. Barnett, S. E. Radio behind walls. Huntsville Prison, Texas, 1936–1940.

34. Ryan, P. R. Theater as prison therapy. *Drama Review*, March 1976, *20*, 31–42.

35. Von Engelhardt, D. Criminal therapy inside and outside prison. *International Journal of Offender Therapy*, 1978, *22*, 201–209.

36. Prittie, T., Artists of Auschwitz: Memorials to misery. *Encounter*, December 1982, *59*, 79–81.

Chapter 15

THE PRISON WRITERS' WORKSHOP

Grady Hillman

For those interested in bringing the wonder of the word to prisons, I must offer some warnings. Given a chance, prison writers' workshops, or any form of fine arts instruction, will have wonderful results. It is getting the chance to go into a penitentiary and teach that is the major obstacle any artist must hurdle.

We think that prisons are in the business of rehabilitating society's errants. That is a myth. Prisons are warehouses for human beings. The function of a prison is to incarcerate and thereby remove a threat from society. That 95 percent of all the people we send to prison will eventually come out is of little concern to correctional officers, and apparently of little concern to the public. The word "rehabilitation" is rarely heard in a penitentiary without an accompanying sneer. Your desire to go into correctional settings for the purpose of reforming convicts into well-adjusted men and women will be greeted with an artificial smile and a runaround.

Guards will view your proposal as just another security headache. To them you will be a naive "free-worlder" come into their prison to foul up the system and create discipline problems; not to mention the bureaucratic hassles of assembling the class— deciding who will be permitted to attend and who will not.

As for the public, there is no mandate that inmates be re-habilitated, only that they be punished. The man on the street views prisons as punitive in nature. Arts programs are often perceived as manifestations of "country clubs." You will hear the litany, "I can't afford lessons for my kid, so why should my taxes buy them for convicts?"

My program in the Texas Department of Corrections began just a few weeks before the Jack Abbott/Norman Mailer fiasco. In the wake of that incident, every correctional writing program in the country found itself under attack. The fact that Abbott never attended a workshop and Mailer never conducted one just didn't register, only that a famous inmate writer committed a heinous crime shortly after his release. I waited for things to cool down a bit, and then queried a magazine on an article on the workshops I was conducting. Here is a portion of the rejection letter:

> I'm sorry, but I've got a prejudice against creative writing programs in prisons. I imagine creative petitions for pardons as the likely result.

That was written by the editor of *American Education,* a magazine published by the Department of Education of the federal government.

So much for the gloom and doom part of this story. I managed to conduct creative writing workshops for 3 years in the Texas Department of Corrections and left of my own volition. In that program I worked with thousands of inmates at 18 different penitentiaries and brought in over a dozen guest artists. For those 3 years, workshops were conducted on three maximum security prison units on a weekly basis. Security gave me a relatively free hand, and the program spawned an award-winning documentary, an anthology, and a great many publications by inmates in the workshops. Having maintained contact with many of the workshop participants after discharge and parole, I can tell you that rehabilitation took place. Very few have gotten into trouble and returned to TDC.

Those of you interested in undertaking this type of project will need some break-in tools.

First, find a vehicle. I was an Artist-in-Education with the

Texas Commission on the Arts and had conducted several creative writing residencies in public schools. Texas is somewhat unique in that it hosts a prison school district. That school district was as eligible for AIE programming as any other district in the state. Knowing they would get me cheap, the prison district applied for a creative writing residency and received it. I was then contracted for my first 10-month stint.

Here I learned one of my first prison lessons: Being under contract to a prison system does not mean you can enter a prison unit. Every warden runs his prison like a feudal lord. If they don't want you on their units, the governor can't get you in. This brings me to my second break-in device: Convince security that you're going to help it do its job. Arts programs reduce tension in prisons; security's task is to maintain order in prisons. There is a common barometer of failure or success and that is the incidence rate, a tally of offenses committed by inmates ranging from fatal stabbings to suicides to simply talking back to a guard. Institution Programs Inc. directs arts residencies for the federal prison system and the Oklahoma Department of Corrections. Fortunately for us they documented the soothing effect of their programs on inmate behavior.

> Statistics were kept at several institutions, recording incidence report data on program participants six months prior to entry up to entry, and during program participation. Meta Metrics, the independent evaluating agency, stated that the incidence rate dropped from over 90% (Womens Unit) to 57% during program participation.

Those are the kinds of figures that will gladden the eye of any warden. A program that will immediately reduce tension among participants is very attractive, and if they are convinced that your program will make things calmer and not result in a radicalized clique, then you are already in.

As for that radicalization process—only once during the time I worked at TDC did a workshop threaten to become an activist organization. It was a particularly tight-knit group, and we'd gotten into a discussion of the ills of the system. (I never censored discussion.) One man, inspired by the talk, a reformer's gleam in his eye, suggested we compose a manifesto and petition the warden, or the governor, or whoever, for change. This proposal sank conversation like a lead balloon and was seconded by silence. Finally, an older convict laconically responded, "Now, Richard. You know this here prison operates on the snitch system, and if we were to do what you ask, well, the warden would know about it before the ink dried on the paper. There's not a man in this workshop I don't like, but there's also not a single one that I trust." This was accepted by the others as a fundamental prison truth, and that was the end of that. I also think that the workshop itself was of such value that they did not want to put it in jeopardy. It was their oasis of free expression, and they were not willing to invite the world in.

Actually, the wardens weren't nearly as fearful of manifestos as they were of another form of writing, the writ. Inmates seeking redressment for abuses will file legal suits against the prison system and its employees. These individuals are called writ writers. When the wardens learned that my fluency in legalese was roughly the same as my knowledge of Sanskrit, their final objection to the workshops was eliminated. I remember one warden asking me flat out if I was going to work with the "writters." Thinking he might be using an East Texas dialect unfamiliar to me, I responded with a hearty, "I sure hope so!" That was not the correct answer. Fortunately, we cleared the matter up, and he graciously accepted my ignorance.

Once I arrived within the walls, difficulty seemed to dissolve. Security rarely bothered me, content to let me operate so long as I didn't tell them how to do their business or "get off into a wreck" by violating some prison rule. For a long time I imagined myself to be under intense scrutiny, but in hindsight, I don't think they were nearly as worried about me as I thought they were then.

My greatest anxiety upon initiating the classes was that the inmates would have already made up their minds about poetry and consider it a "sissified" business. What I found was the exact opposite. An experienced guess puts the poetry writing prison population at about 40 percent. And those that can't write often pay others to do it for them. There are inmates who've earned more in cigarettes and coffee than I ever made in dollars selling poetry. The reason should have been obvious to me. Almost everyone in prison has a husband or wife, a lover or mother, some special person on the outside who the inmate hopes will wait for them. With no contact visits available, no meetings more than twice a month and those behind thick glass screens, the love poem has been resurrected. A poem can have the persuasive power of a kiss and can intoxicate as easily as an embrace, but its effects last much longer. To write a love poem for someone evinces extreme affection and certain flattery. The love poem, though of romantic birth, is as utilitarian in prison as legal books or the "stingers" inmates use to heat water for coffee. Skill in the art is a prized vocation.

This is the most common use of poetry in prison, but there are others just as important. I asked the members of my workshops why they had turned to writing poetry, and their responses tell us much about prisons and poetry. I would like to illustrate the following points with samples of their work.

Poetry writing provides a means of expressing the softer emotions in an environment where tenderness is perceived as weakness. It is a private act that does not invite exploitation by others. The "hardened criminal" is more metaphor than cliché. Men and women behind bars must put on masks of insensitivity to survive. Yet worn too long, the masks become real, and institutionalization achieves the wrong end of destroying the right feelings.

Idyll

A man in a dingy, grey-blue suit
sarcastically handed
you to me
tonight
and a great knowing smile
silently appeared upon my
    face—
joy you may never understand.

I gently carried you,
walking the long aisle
to my bed
and together we lay down.

I'd already fixed
a cup of steaming hot coffee,
lit a not-often-had freeworld,
readied for the enjoyment
of spending time alone with
    you.

Putting headset on,
tuned a C&W station,
where another Jones was
    singing
about someone's lonely past—
I'm in the middle of you
and yes, I too rather
we were there together,
than you, me—this letter.

Andrew McCord Jones

Poetry writing provides a means for self-reflection. In TDC the inmates all wore the same uniform, had the same GI haircut, and as far as the system was concerned, differed only in the numbers they wore on their chests. Through writing they were able to maintain a sense of personal identity, of uniqueness. Only through this self-knowledge can any true healing take place. The following poem by Lonnie Griggs, while fatalistic in tone, exemplifies this reflective process.

Pop's Proverb*

the morning is moist
but not wet enough for flatweeding
so we pull carrots
in a field gone to seed

i pull those gnarled monstrosities
musing about myself

---

*Previously published in the *Texas Observer*.

and all the guys
i've known here since reform school
now gray bent wrinkled
but carrying on still
ever doing our little numbers
because something inside us
lay in the field too long
and grew somehow twisted

a young drive-up saunters up
mutters 'what it is pop?'
i scrap a glob moist red clay
from an obscene carrot
squeeze it through my fingers
and say distinctly
son it ain't shit

i watch his eyes
and see he doesn't realize
he's just received
all my wisdom
and all the philosophy
he'll likely ever need
as he boogies on down the row
i toss an ugly carrot in the crate
reach for another
and hum beneath my breath
the old blues song that says
it's a doggone lowdown dirty shame

Lonnie Griggs

Another reason for writing is the aforementioned release of tension which security likes so well. Prisons are harsh and monotonous, and the human pressures that naturally build can literally kill. An outburst of sudden anger can result in the loss of "good time" and a stay in segregation meaning a few more months until discharge or parole. Attacking a guard or fellow inmate on paper is much more helpful than the real thing and serves the same purpose of blowing off steam.

Dearly Beloved Guardians

If I were fed your kindly thoughts
I would starve within a week;
If all I spoke were your golden smiles
Then I would never speak.

If I could smell your gentle heart,
Sewage would sell in flasks.
So when you come to speak of truth
Leave behind your grinning mask.

Jorge Antonio Renaud

The last two reasons they gave me for writing poetry are somewhat entwined, so I'd like to present them together. Inmates use verse for its escape value and as a mnemonic device to preserve memory. The creation of images in fantasy or the reliving of images found in memory serve the same purpose of displacing the immediate environment and transporting the consciousness elsewhere. If you can't jump the fences, why not travel in your mind. Convicts who served longer sentences, more than 5 years, take this process one step further. Without the stimulus of reminders such as laughing children, female voices, certain textures, smells, and colors, they find that the memory begins to lose its integrity. Fantasy gains a foothold. They ask themselves if what they remember really took place, or was the experience a product of the imagination. At this point the recording of memories in poems, and a reliance on the memory for poetic images infuses strength and stability into the writer's recollections. By exercising the memory on paper it regains health.

Such a Dreamer*

I'm riding in my new Ford pickup
Cathe sitting so close I can smell her hair
I love the smell of her clean freshly shampooed hair

---

*Previously published in *Writer's Block: An Anthology of Texas Prison Writing*.

Wind along the river
blows freely through our souls
It's spring
and spring invades our every fiber

I make plans
Cathe mischievously smiles
and her eyes sparkle brighter with every word
can't help but laugh
She knows I'm such a dreamer

Mile upon mile
We're really not going anywhere
just going together
past cane pole wielding children
past river camps
past the dotted farms on the Mississippi bottoms

past our every fear
past our every worry

WATER TIME 5 HOE yells the prison guard

I come back
back to this prison farm
back to this cotton field
and back to reality

I lay down my hoe on the row I'm working
and walk past the horse-riding guard to my water

I'm smiling

Don't go away Cathe dearest
I'll be right back!

Joseph M. Depauw

Chapter 16

WINDOWS

Betty Vreeman

. . . I stood on one side of a chasm and she on the other. There was no bridge. I tried to build one. "How are you. . . really?"

"Fine," said my friend. Her eyes were tired and her face was thin.

"And your family?"

"We're well," she said. Even across the chasm I could see her lie. I love her. I have missed her. I remember those days when there was no chasm, when we shared the joys and tears friends share together. Now we are adults, and we have destroyed our bridges and created our chasms. We do not cross them any longer. So there was nothing left to say. And no way to say it if there had been.

It is that way with everyone. It happened with the boy who took me riding when the autumn leaves fell on our faces and the world was larger than the two of us. Since then I have seen him across the chasm, but what we shared had separated like petals from a flower and each of us, saving the petals, could not remember the blossom. Or would not.

I met two friends the other day. "How wonderful to see you again," I said. "How are you?"

"Just fine," they said. "And you?"

"Oh, so much has happened," I said. "I wish. . ."

And they said, "We must get together for a long talk." And

all around us were the cold winds of the canyon and then they were gone. It wasn't my fault. It wasn't theirs. Perhaps I cry for the lost dream and deny found reality, but it seems to me that the earth is a path we walk together with those we meet and love. If the paths must part from time to time, must they always meet on opposite sides of chasm?

The world is a lonely place sometimes. How do you build a bridge?

Poor communication is rightly blamed for many of our social, political, educational, and business conflicts. Pick up any newspaper or magazine and you will read somewhere that ineffective or "poor" communication is the cause for employer-employee conflicts; decreasing credibility of local, state, and national politicians; student-administration problems; family breakups and quarrels which sometimes lead to violent crimes; and on and on—more and more examples of higher and stronger barriers between people.

Anthropologists Toeffler and Tournier describe our twentieth century mobile society as lonely; they tell us that although we meet more people in a year than our nineteenth century ancestors did in their lifetimes, we are less and less deeply involved with others—and we make only superficial contact, if any, with most people we meet.

Psychiatrists and psychologists document the fact that the numbers behind mental illness in the United States is not substance abuse alone, but loneliness and depression—caused by the inability to communicate and relate effectively with other people. Slater (1970, 1974) goes so far as to say that people in America are actually conducting a "pursuit of loneliness" and that this has brought our culture to the breaking point. A recent *New York Times* service feature was picked up by newspapers in every major city; in it loneliness is identified as "a national epidemic"—perhaps the number one disease in the country!

Dory Previn sings:

> I think perhaps tomorrow
> I'll try to make a friend
> To really get
> To know him

Instead of pretend
I'll ask him if his feet hurt
Has he burdens to be
   shared
And if he doesn't walk
   away
I'll ask him
If he's scared
And if he doesn't walk
   away
If his eyes don't
Turn to stone
I'll ask him
If he's scared
To be alone

Why are people lonely? Many human relations experts say people are lonely because they prefer to live behind barriers—they build walls instead of windows. Even though they spend all of their waking hours in some form of communication, they are afraid or don't know how to establish effective contact with people in their personal or professional lives.

How do we help people build bridges across chasms and windows instead of walls? The key is communication. The word "communicate," like communion and community, is built on the root word meaning "one." When two people communicate, they are trying to make a new "one." What was two before now becomes one. When you and I communicate, we have created a new being composed of the two of us. That is why I define communication as "creation." The new "one" created by our communicating never existed before. It is a new creation—just as the putting together of two pigments forms a new color; just as the putting together of separate notes becomes a chord or melody—so we create as we communicate. From this first step in "one-making," the process is endless. Every new "one" can communicate with a second "one" to create a newer "one." This is the eternal process of human creation. This is drama. It is communication—*one-making*. It can cross chasms and build or open windows.

This drama is not something we can take or leave. For humans it is as indispensable as breathing. There are documented cases of people becoming physically ill and even dying from loneliness and lack of communication. How can we make this creation process—effective communication—happen? Any form of creative and effective communication must have the following concepts: First, you the communicator, must care for and understand yourself. You must have and convey self-confidence, pride in yourself as a worthwhile individual. Without this first attitude and belief, you cannot achieve the second which is that you, the communicator, care for and understand others. You are aware of the other person(s) as unique individuals with their own hopes and dreams and ideas; you respond to them as well as "hear" them—you convey your concern and understanding. Finally, you the communicator, must be able to express yourself (verbally and nonverbally) adequately and effectively to others and be able to receive and act upon expressions from them. This sounds almost impossible for educators and therapists and leaders in all fields to accomplish—maybe even more impossible for people who have come to us for help?

And what does all this have to do with creative arts therapy? It has *everything* to do with it, because participation in creative arts experiences—creative, dramatic expression from within—is concerned with developing and stimulating our dramatic instinct. And our dramatic instinct helps us open windows on life and between each other. Success in every walk of life depends on our dramatic instinct.

The teacher cannot teach unless he sees as the student sees. The preacher cannot preach without the power of putting himself in another man's place. The merchant succeeds by his ability to read the wishes and needs of his customers. This is how it is throughout all human experience and endeavor—an instinctive knowledge of human nature is the basis of success. All men are "great" in proportion to their ability to get outside themselves. A person who has killed his dramatic, creative instinct has become unsympathetic and can never appreciate anyone's point of view but his own. It is this dramatic instinct which gives deep insight into the motives and needs and desires of other people.

This dramatic instinct is, and has always been, a prime force in civilization. The need to give voice to pent-up emotion, to express joy in living, to put into material form the ideas and experiences that affect his spirit has always driven man to create. Ancient peoples satisfied this in songs and pantomime; the Egyptians and Assyrians showed some of their dramatic, creative instinct in their temple bas-reliefs; Oriental civilizations created puppet performances and storytelling; ancient Hebrews had their religious dances and grand dramatic odes; Greeks celebrated with processions, festivals, and theater; every culture communicated its ideas and experiences through one of the creative arts. In fact, all of the "arts" can be considered communications from people in the past, or even the present. Perhaps this is why participating in creative arts experiences can be so beneficial, so therapeutic for all of the participants.

Since effective communication depends on self-confidence, experiences which develop that self-confidence are essential in any kind of therapy or work in developing better human relations and self-expression. I believe some of the best windows on life and bridges between people are opened and built through use of creative arts. Today I am talking about creative drama which is a combination art form: it involves all the oral, nonverbal, and visual forms of communication at one time or another, separately or together. Creative drama is a total participation process based on stimulating and developing that dramatic instinct through creating and experiencing drama—dance, movement, mime, poetry, media, the visual arts, and all of the combinations, because these arts can be a vital part of helping people communicate with and relate effectively to themselves as well as others.

Using the creative drama process, and incorporating creative arts activities, experiences, and concepts and techniques will help develop those abilities. Using your own imagination and a variety of physical, mental, emotional, and social skills to see yourself, others, and your inner and outer environments in new and different ways will open and build new windows and new worlds for those of us who participate, as either leader or group member. What are some of the specific goals or objectives for using these creative arts concepts, ideas, and activities in your work with individuals or groups, particularly in therapeutic settings? We have to remember that the purpose of this kind of "drama" is *not* the training of actors, or the producing of plays for an audience. The purposes are more like these:

> to develop confidence in self and a person's own ability to communicate and relate effectively; to give a chance to each person to find an avenue of self-expression in one of the arts (not just music, visual art, or writing).

> to provide insight into self and group "individuality" and personalities—along with learning some techniques for functioning effectively (and happily) in a variety of settings with various people.

> to provide a controlled emotional outlet. There are positive ways to express emotions of all kinds.

> to encourage and guide and develop creative imagination and emphathic powers. We've already talked about the necessity and importance of developing the imagination. It is that "magic force" that goes beyond mastery of facts and techniques in the search for new ideas.

> to provide opportunities for creative problem solving. Problem solving is both subjective and objective. Part of growing up fully and creatively is discovering the great variety of processes by which we assess, evaluate, form opinions, make decisions.

> to provide opportunities for growth in cooperation and social understanding. In creative dramatic experiences the group has to cooperate; they have to come to workable compromises in any problem situation in which all can take part according to individual capabilities and experiences; they learn to become aware of the group feeling and direction; they learn to take responsibility for their ideas as a whole—"We've done it!"—not "I've done it!"

> to give experience in thinking on "your feet" and expressing ideas clearly and fearlessly. Older people report that besides being enjoyable, creative dramatic activities help them with poise and confidence. Oral communication is a *must* in our society: people who are learning to respect their own thoughts and feelings and to express ideas to each other are at the same time becoming more sensitive

to thoughts and feelings of others, and are on the road to real communication.

If creative, dramatic experiences are well guided and planned there are many other objectives that can be realized; such as initiative, resourcefulness, freedom in bodily expression, better speech habits and many others. In short, the purpose of using creative arts in therapy is to help people discover themselves and a whole new process for living confidently and joyfully. The most obvious, almost immediate, result in people who participate in this process—from the profoundly handicapped to intellectual professionals—is a dramatic improvement and demonstration of self-confidence and self-expression.

The creative arts have been a vital part of my own personal life since the age of three, and the central force in my professional/working life since my first job at age thirteen. Once I started working with professionals in a wide variety of disciplines and realized the positive effects of creative arts experiences—especially in building self-confidence and in interpersonal skills—I went out of my way to experiment in as many different situations with as many different people as I could. I've worked (or played) with groups—using creative arts—in a variety of physical spaces including hospital rooms and wards, libraries, dormitory rooms, huge gyms, living rooms, commercial Greyhound buses, airports, airplanes, ferry-crossings in Africa, personnel departments, waiting rooms, interstate highway rest areas, and my own office as well as the more usual conference spaces. The results, no matter what the space or the individual or the group, were remarkably similar. The proofs, in pictures and videotapes, are "worth a thousand words." Further testimony is offered by people who went through the process.

"I think I'll have some confidence in front of people now; more than I had before. I saw how relaxing and feeling good got rid of my nervousness and a lot of those bad habits I knew I had, but didn't know how to get rid of. I don't know if you intended this, but I've decided to call a girl I've been wanting to get to know for a long time—and I'm sure it's going to go okay—and that's a big admission for me. . . .

". . . I began to conquer some of my fears about relating to other people, and became a little more confident and poised. One thing this experience taught me was that many of the things I worried about in my appearance were needless—why did it take me so long?"

". . . I think the best part of this experience was the environment that was created. Everyone was encouraged to look at all the positive qualities of everybody else and everyone was accepted for what they were and not what someone else wanted them to be. It was like living in a Don Quixote world. It seemed like people were always looking towards what we could be if we were really uplifted and loved."

". . . But most important, the experience helped me gain self-confidence. Through the trust and sharing sessions especially, I have learned my fears are shared by almost everyone . . . this makes it easier to work with others. . ."

"I feel confident and I know that's the key to even more progress; I hope this feeling stays because it's easy to experiment when you feel good."

"This experience with the arts focused me on discovering my strengths and weaknesses . . . with better self-knowledge I feel more self-confident and capable right now; I also learned it's OK to take a risk—valuable, in fact! I always hope as a leader to instill a sense of self-directed knowledge-seeking in my group members. But perhaps most important, by my own example, I now hope to show that it is OK to care about others as well as yourself."

"I think I relaxed with my peers for the first time in a long while. I feel like I'm more expressive, and they all told me I was so I've got to believe it. I think I'll go meet a few more strangers tonight!"

". . . I was afraid and wanted to not continue after the first couple of hours. I am self-conscious and distrustful as a general rule and I realized I wasn't going to get by with that. I'm glad as a person that can care and give and also about trusting and believing in others."

". . . The most beneficial exercises to me were the ones where we could be the 'craziest.' When I realized how easy and fun it is to 'let go' I wanted to keep experimenting. I think I'll say more of what I'm really thinking from now on—I discovered it's worth the risk."

". . . Words aren't really adequate to express how much I enjoyed this. I wish I could write a poem or compose a song or paint a picture about it right now!"

"I learned more about myself and what I need to do to improve my communication skills than I ever could have imagined. This wasn't a goal of mine for this workshop, but the result is a major blessing to me. My chief goal was to become a "freer" person: even my colleagues joke about my inhibitions in our group meetings. I know I'm on the right track after this experience, even though I also know it will take a lot of practice. I found out I don't have to worry about other people's reactions so much—we're all scared!"

". . . I found the role-playing techniques and exercises most beneficial for me in my 'career.' But personally I really appreciated the 'warm-up' things like toe and finger-dancing; they helped me understand and express feelings that are usually difficult for me to express."

"I think the arts experience will benefit me in all my people-contacts—church, home, work, whatever. You're right about always having room for one more good friend, but I never believed it before—easier to keep the old relationships the same way. But I think I've gained the courage (and certainly some techniques) to "go out of my way" to engage in some new communication experiences."

I wish I could share more of the poems and stories and dances and skits and circus parades and side shows and scarf dances and reactions of the people who led and participated in this process—this drama—these experiences in creative arts which became therapy for the body, and mind, and heart, and soul, with everyone building windows instead of walls. I hope therapists will consider adding a dramatic, creative "arts" dimension to their "best" therapeutic techniques, and enjoy the new bridges and windows they and their clients or groups will discover. This little poem by e.e. cummings[1] will take on a new, practical meaning:

> Now I love you and you love me
> (and books are shutter
> than books
> can be)

and deep in the high that does nothing but fall
(with a shout
each
around we go all)
there's somebody calling who's *we*
We're anything brighter than even the sun
(we're everything greater
than books
might mean)
We're everything more than believe
(with a spin
leap
alive we're alive)
We're wonderful one times one!

REFERENCE

1. cummings, e.e. *Complete poems, 1913–1962.* New York: Harcourt Brace Javonovich, 1972, p. 324.

Chapter 17

THE USE OF POETRY IN PSYCHIATRY

John F. Whitaker

There are counterindications, risks, and counterproductive uses of poetry and poetry therapy. Low stress tolerance and poor ego boundaries without adequate interpersonal resources for reality testing is a possible counterindication. In particular, this includes some borderline personality disorders (DSM-III criteria), schizophrenic and bipolar (manic-depressive) disorders, and certain organically impaired patients. Also, there are some intact individuals with extraordinary overwhelming life stresses who may experience damaging effects from poetry.

Moreover, as with other gratification-producing experiences, there is a risk of poetry being used to avoid problem solving. These individuals may write poetry but not change their behavior. People without clear definitions of self, such as evolving adolescents, may be at risk by identifying with the disturbed mental state of some writers. Many adolescent drug abusers and suicide victims may have been influenced by poetry in such music as presents intense disorganized conflict without ordered resolution. There are advertisers who use poetic techniques which promote the abusive and addictive use of food, alcohol, tobacco, and even legal drugs. In my experience, creative people who use drugs and/or alcohol to pharmacologically disinhibit left hemispheric brain function and enhance right hemispheric brain experience can be at increased risk for damaging mistakes due to impaired judgment, illnesses, psychotic episodes, social and physical suicide, murder, and accidental death. The reader can think of examples of prominent creative people today and in history who have suffered, gone insane, and died under these circumstances. So the protective parental message warning us not to let our emotions rule us still applies; but do not rule out emotions either, because emotions are necessary for health and a sense of full aliveness.

However, in my work at the Whitaker Psychiatric Medical Center in Dallas, Texas, I have not personally witnessed any of the above deleterious effects of poetry therapy.

Indeed, the following examples, drawn from my practice as a psychiatrist using individual counseling and psychotherapy, family and marital therapy, group psychotherapy, and in my workshops confirm the constructive role of poetry. Except for the unedited sample poem, *Carla's Baby,* the following case examples are composites and fictionalized to protect confidentiality.

Carla, a thirty-four-year-old attractive single female diagnosed as a case of dysthymic disorder (depressive neurosis) and borderline personality disorder had sat in our group psychotherapy sessions for several months before sharing her emotional self. She did not become a real part of the group until she wrote a poem saying good-bye to her daughter who was almost sixteen. She has surrendered her child for adoption shortly after birth and had never seen her again. Her writing triggered torrents of tears and racking sobs. As she reached the last stanza she "healed into peaceful acceptance." The following is her poem:

Carla's Baby

The baby's grown up now.
She's almost sixteen.
Not a seven-year-old
Who is pink at the seams.

"Where are you living?
Who are Mom and Dad?

Are you bright and happy?
Are your days long and sad?"

Was it yesterday when
The labor pains came?
I remember the winds
Of a hurricane.

It's two fifty-five
on a Sunday in Fall
A swat on the bottom,
A loud healthy bawl.

"What is it?" I asked.
"Oh, please let me see.
She's beautiful," I cried.
"She looks just like me."

So long ago when . . .
I held for three hours
A small baby girl . . .
She's now their "ours."

She's still in my heart,
In my mind and my soul.
I will let her go,
Take back my control.

Cry? Yes a lot
And mourn for her loss.
She'll never be with me;
I'll put down my cross.

A tear's in my soul
For the baby who's gone.
It's over at last;
I don't have to be strong.

Go on with your living;
Forgive if you can.

Afraid and alone,
I gave birth and ran.

"Wishing for Miracles"
I give up today.
Love and warm memories
To keep; Yes, they'll stay.

At one repressed level, Carla had identified with her own mother who had never released her from a symbiotic relationship allowing her to separate, individuate, and grow autonomously. As she completed the grief for her baby, by regression she and the mother part of herself grieved and completed separations long overdue from very early ages. Unable at first to share herself directly with the group, she did so with poetry. She then experienced a nurturing acceptance and support that she had never before known. With this breakthrough she began to share herself directly and spontaneously with other group members. As others felt moved by her work to share themselves in return she no longer felt so alone and different. The other group participants also worked on their conflict areas of separation, individuation, and letting go of their own children. As she continued to write poetry her interest turned from themes of finding, knowing, and loving herself to love for others, marriage, and family. In a sense her poems served as waking dreams, and her dreams given form through poetry became a reality. When I last heard from her I learned that she was married to a loving husband, had two healthy children, and was continuing to advance in her career.

A twenty-nine-year-old single chronic undifferentiated schizophrenic, Lonnie, with no close relationships, wrote poetry almost daily for many years. With the help of psychotropic medication he maintained partial remission of his illness as his writing provided a safety-valve for tumultuous emotions. Sharing his poetry served as a crucial means for making contact with others and acted to keep his thinking oriented to reality and so organized that he could be understood by others. It was also a primary source of structuring leisure time. Thus he achieved a vital sense of mastery and self-esteem from his writing. Lonnie supported himself with regular employment in a large corporation and avoided hospitalizations. Despite the severity of his illness he maintained a remarkable level of functioning.

Another case illustrating the valuable role of poetry to therapy is that of Nadine. She suffered from recurrent major depressions and a compulsive personality disorder. She had suffered from overwhelming life stress. When she was forty-one, her fourteen-year-old son began using drugs. He ran away from home and broke off all communication. Soon afterwards, her husband was killed in an automobile accident. She was overwhelmed and spent weeks in isolation drinking heavily. With glazed eyes staring into the nothingness of her future, she placed a 32-caliber pistol just behind her right ear and pulled the trigger. Miraculously, the bullet ricocheted in her head, lodging in her maxillary sinus and sparing the vital areas of her brain. When she recovered it was with minimal brain damage and a deafness in her right ear. Some months later, she developed breast cancer and was compelled to undergo a bilateral radical mastectomy. Throughout this agonizing experience she had never cried.

She became a workaholic. Suffering from recurrent suicidal thinking she controlled her depression with antidepressent medication. During early sessions in psychotherapy she refused to communicate feelings at any depth. In the waiting room she read the bulletin board where patients could share their poems. (It is my practice also to display therapeutic poems which I have written on major conflict areas.) I had just posted a poem on suicide, which connected words with the feelings of the suicidal position and its resolution. Reading the poem pushed emotional buttons. She entered the therapy room crying. She grieved for her adult losses and for a young girl whose mother had never wanted her. During the following year she worked through a "mountain" of grief. When her feelings had been blocked or when she was in need of extra support she listened to appropriate music or read favorite poems and passages from the Bible. In this way she strengthened her decision to live. When she found herself free of depression and suicidal ideation, Nadine left therapy in a process of continuing growth.

Vance, a forty-year-old attorney, married and with four children, had come for marital therapy with his thirty-two-year-old wife, Darlene. She was dangerously overweight. Her primary roles were those of homemaker and schoolteacher. He was afflicted with a severe generalized anxiety associated with feelings of inadequacy and a fear of failure. He also suffered sexual performance anxiety and became impotent and subsequently withdrew from contact with his wife. He deflected his interest to daily jogging; she chose food. For him feelings of power, achievement, and success were associated with terrifying disasters in his childhood. His family lost everything when his father, at the height of his career, was sent to prison. Subsequently, the father committed suicide.

As an adjunct to therapy, I asked him to become aware of the enduring power in Nature and write a poem about his experience. As he wrote of the oceans, mountains, atoms, universe, and God, he felt the power, his power.

He kept the poem with him and resorted to it time and again whenever he felt anxiety-ridden. A scotch-taped copy of the poem was attached to his bathroom mirror so that it could speak to him each morning as he shaved. While his confidence and communication skills continued to develop both he and Darlene found themselves helpless and confused about one of their sons. Because of the psychological problems of Vance and Darlene the boy was so affected that he became a discipline problem at school and began to fail in his studies. I encouraged the family to come to my parenting workshop. Among other techniques I employ is one where I present a poem I have written and set to music, in order to inspire goal setting and feelings of achievement. The use of tone, rhythm, rhyme, and metaphor are valuable tools in teaching. Vance memorized the song, and the family sang it on their car trips. As Vance helped his son overcome anxiety, he helped himself, and he and his wife grew closer.

Darlene kept a journal which had always remained private. She decided to risk sharing it with Vance. He found her trust and intimate disclosures deeply moving. They felt a reawakening of the love they had experienced years before. She enjoyed writing as an adjunct to her therapy, and so wrote unmailed letters to her mother, father, and sister, as a means of gaining closure of those relationships. She began to lose weight. The sensual, attractive woman he had known in their courting days emerged out of a cocoon of adipose tissue. She wrote Vance a simple love poem for a Valentine's card. They made love.

"Therapeutic poetry" is not just for those who choose to grow in a psychiatric setting, it is for all people. I wrote *Unmask* as "therapeutic poetry" to work with women in the liberation movement of the 1970s. I have used it as a stimulus for communication and problem solving in groups and in intensive psychotherapy. *Unmask's* poetic power focuses past the embroidery on specific key conflict areas and promotes selective therapeutic regression by speaking in simple "life-rhymes" to the childlike parts. It facilitates integration at the mature adult level.

As an adjunct to marital therapy, I wrote the book *Personal Marriage Contract.* The factually oriented expository style was less effective than the poetic prose and the simple, harmonious style of writing, which evoked more emotional experience while conveying information. Couples reported significant therapeutic benefits from reading the book aloud and using it as a springboard for communication.

I identified observable components of what my patients designated as "love." I wrote poetry to expand the meaning of these ten *Skill-Action Areas of Loving,* which are: Withness and the dependence/independence/interdependence issues; friends and one's social support system; time and its management; work and play activities; rights and assertiveness; "strokes" and meeting recognition needs; nurturing and healthy dependency; sex and maintenance of romantic love; quarrels and expression of feelings; and contracts and trust. Poetry catalyzed awareness and growth. Many felt inspired to write their own poetry. They often found that sharing the poetry of love created an intense level of intimacy. Here is an example written for the first skill-action area:

Withness

Man and woman in motion and rhythm,
Touch and love in life's natural system.
As the dancing of the sky with the Earth,
Motion and marriage give clouds and trees birth.

They give to each the flow of life's fountain,
From stream to sea, and from cloud to mountain.
Dancing together free through lifetimes of time.
Apart and unique, yet both intertwine.

The Sky touches Earth's Sea with its sunburst,
And warmed from the sun, Sea quenches Sky's thirst.
Man and woman in motion and rhythm,
Drink warmth of Earth and touch starts of Heaven.

A cloud dissolves and trees wither and die,
Yet living on are the Earth and the Sky.
Man and woman in motion and rhythm,
Touch and love in God's natural system.

© *John F. Whitaker, M.D.*

As a response to the popularity of writing in therapy, I started a creativity workshop. In the workshop's introduction, I quote from my book *Unmask:* "Experience the powerful therapeutic force of poetry as a vehicle for self-discovery and growth. Poetry invites the conscious emergence of repressed conflict and emotions, and facilitates freeing energy for expansion to new levels of awareness, intelligence, and experience." I explain that the purpose of therapeutic writing is to illuminate unfelt feelings, hidden meanings, and unseen relationships. Poetry can be a sublime frolic of lovers through a sea of wild flowers or an inspirational march to victory over a formidable foe. It can be a pleasant superficial walk around the block, or an in-depth journey to the endless ends of our minds. Seeking and finding each new line is an adventure of exploration through the process of free association, one of the most effective psychotherapeutic techniques. It can be terrifying, despairing, angering, exhilarating, and soothing.

In the adventurous journey of in-depth exploration, the writer is repeatedly stopped momentarily, or for prolonged periods by the repressive barrier. The adventurer must struggle with writer's block and somehow find the courage and the means to overcome numerous possible resistances. In tunneling through the barriers, the writer may unleash grotesque monsters, trap himself between impenetrable rocks, fall into bottomless pits, trigger explosions, and tap into torrents of drowning floods. There may be a disordering of cherished beliefs and securely structured thinking which can evoke anxiety and conjure up early feelings prior to the reordering of thought. He must confront infantile terrors of abandonment and grieve through the infantile experience of perceived loss of parental approval and love to reach the joy of knowing and integrating the forbidden fruit from the tree of knowledge. As resolution and completion of the gestalt forms the finished work, the writer finds that all is well and even better than ever back home after adventuring in the Land of Oz.

The growth process/creative process/psychotherapeutic process requires a connection and integration of both intellectual and emotional insight. Words are keys to unlock doors into these dual insight levels so that one does not just "think" or just "feel" a truth; one "knows." When writing therapeutic poetry to be read by patients in bibliotherapy, I frequently switch back and forth between the two.

I have found poetry to be a powerful psychotherapeutic modality. The poetic communication style invites integration of the functions of the right and the left hemispheres of the brain. Poetry speaks to the imagery, intuitive, and emotional aspects of the right hemisphere as it speaks to the mathematical, logical, and linguistic functions of the left. It is a blending of art and science. Writing, reading, reciting, and listening to poetry enable individuals to be aware of the universality of human experience and help to delineate individual uniqueness. Poetry speaks to the conscious and the unconscious mind simultaneously. By activation of hormonal and neuronal systems every cell in the body is biochemically and physiologically affected. Moreover, through the connectiveness promoted by communication with others, poetry is a highly effective social psychotherapeutic vehicle. It traverses the intrapsychic, interpersonal and spiritual dimensions of human existence. Consequently, poetry therapy satisfies the complete biopsychosocial model of psychiatric treatment.

BIBLIOGRAPHY

Butcher, S. H. *Theory of poetry and fine art*, New York: Dover, 1951.

Leedy, J. J. (Ed.) *Poetry therapy: The use of poetry in the treatment of emotional disorders*. Philadelphia, PA: Lippincott & Co., 1969.

Leedy, J. J. *Poetry, the healer*. Philadelphia, PA. Lippincott & Co., 1972.

Meerloo, J. A. N. Archaic behavior and the communicative act. *Psychiatric Quarterly*, 1955, *29*, 60.

Pietropinto, A. Poetry therapy in groups. In J. Masserman (Ed.), *Current psychiatric therapies*. New York: Grune & Stratton, 1975.

Whitaker, J. F. *Personal marriage contract*. Dallas, Texas: OK Street, Inc., 1976.

Whitaker, J. F. *Ummask*. Dallas, Texas: OK Street, Inc., 1977.

AFTERWORD

Those who labor in the vineyards of poetry therapy and the associated modalities are not only descendants of an ancient tradition but are in a sense pioneers, since they are part of a scientific brotherhood as well as men of intuition and would not be unhappy with scientific validation of their theories and procedures. For them this statement intended by Carl J. Jung for his colleagues in another, a possibly related area, that of psychic research, may be regarded as equally fitting:

The pioneer in a new field rarely has the good fortune to be able to draw valid conclusions from his total experience. The efforts and exertions, the doubts and uncertainties of this voyage of discovery have penetrated his marrow too deeply to allow the perspective and clarity which are necessary for a comprehensive presentation. Those of the second generation—who base their work on his groping attempts, the chance hits, the circuitous approaches, the half-truths and mistakes of the pioneer—are less burdensome and can take more direct roads, envisage further goals. They are able to cast off many doubts and hesitations, concentrate on essentials, and in this way, map out a simpler and clearer picture of the newly discovered territory. The simplification and clarification redound to the benefit of those of the third generation who are thus equipped from the onset with an overall chart. With this chart they are enabled to formulate new problems and mark out the boundaries more sharply than ever before.

Not many of the subtle and intricate transmutations that occur in patient and therapist after the introduction of poetry into the therapeutic session are as yet measurable.

Yet lest in our anxiety for a validation of poetry therapy, we base all on "scientific proof" alone, we should, I believe, keep the following in mind. In the realm of physics, Heisenberg has advised us that "science no longer confronts us as an objective observer but sees itself as an actor in this interplay between man and nature." We have clearly progressed from the Newtonian world which was absolute, continuous, material, and causal, and moved into the universe of Einstein, Planck, and Bohr which is characterized by relativity, discontinuity, energy, and statistics. Scientific study can no longer be viewed as based on objectivity and certainty but must confess to an inescapable subjectivity and uncertainty.

From the field of psychiatry we find this observation recorded by Dr. Jules Masserman, Professor Emeritus of Psychiatry and Neurology at Northwestern School of Medicine, and former president of the American Psychiatric Association:

"Although currently evolving systems—dynamic orientations and correspondingly multi-faceted and effective modes of treatment, *psychiatry, as many other disciplines, retains many aspects of mysticism.*"[1]

Dr. Carl Simonton served formerly as chief of radiation therapy at David Grant USAF Medical Center, Travis Air Force Base (1971–1982) and is presently engaged in cancer research, evaluating the role played by such factors as the will to live versus the will to die, the physiological aspects of meditation, etc. In a paper entitled *The Role of the Mind in Cancer Therapy,*[2] he discusses the case histories of patients who responded successfully to his treatment and relates the following:

"One topic I am frequently required to address is that of medical or scientific proof. Before I began this study and had only the ideas, most of my colleagues told me that I would never be able to prove anything because there were too many variables involved. As I have accumulated more and more results, I still find that the question of scientific proof is a very difficult one. About a week ago I came across an article which meant a great deal to me, and I would like to share it with you.

"The article was about a psychiatrist who was doing some rather unorthodox work with schizophrenic patients approximately 20 years ago and was obtaining some very good results. Because of the nature of his techniques, however, his colleagues were reluctant to listen to him. He wrote approximately 10 articles on the subject, but their standard response was, "Well, you really haven't proven anything." So he continued his work and wrote about 10 more articles, and people continued to say the same thing. He began to wonder just what it is that constitutes scientific proof. He did still more work and published more papers, with the same result. He became determined to investigate thoroughly this question of scientific proof.

"Being the editor of a psychiatric journal, he decided to hold a symposium on the subject. He wrote letters to several leading scientists asking for their participation in a study to determine what constitutes scientific proof. The first reply came from a man who sent a very short note: 'The question,' he wrote, 'is much too difficult for me.' He went on to say, briefly, that he doubted that he could make a significant contribution to so complex an issue.

"This answer was more than the humility of a great man; it was more than the reflection of scientific honesty. It was at the root of a great man's whole philosophy of being. The letter was signed, 'Albert Einstein.' "

When Freud was asked by Einstein whether psychoanalysis was essentially a mythology, Freud replied, "But are not all sciences?"

REFERENCES

1. Masserman, J. H., The comparative scientific status of psychiatry. *The American Journal of Social Psychiatry*, Winter 1982, *11*(1).

2. Simonton, C. The role of the mind in cancer therapy. In S. Dean (Ed.), *Psychiatry and mysticism*. Chicago: Nelson Hall, 1975.

BIBLIOGRAPHY

Dean, S. R. Metapsychiatry: The confluence of psychiatry and mysticism. *Fields within Fields*, Spring 1974.

Harding, E. G. *Psychic energy: Its source and its transformation*. New York: Pantheon Books, 1963.

McNiff, S. *The arts and psychotherapy*. Springfield, IL: Charles C. Thomas, 1981.

Stade, G. *Robert Graves*. New York: Columbia University Press, 1967.

Appendix A

QUESTIONS AND ANSWERS

The following are questions and answers that have characterized the interchange between platform and audience at past symposia on the use of poetry in healing. Sponsors included such organizations as The American Psychiatric Association, The American Association for Social Psychiatry, The American Academy for Psychoanalysis, The National Association for Poetry Therapy, The American Academy for Poetry Therapy.

Question:

What is poetry therapy?

Answer:

Because poetry is the most evocative, most magical, most penetrating means of human communication, it has become recognized in therapeutic circles as a highly valued resource for effecting desired changes in attitudes, thoughts, and conduct among those suffering from emotional distress and maladaptive behavior. The reading and writing of poetry is being assigned a prominent place both in individual and group therapies. It is a unique modality but has its psychological parallels in the creative experiences provided in art, music, and dance therapy. It is essentially a form of psychotherapy based on the same principles as are other forms of therapy. It differs from them since it introduces as an additional force into the therapeutic encounter, the voice of the poet.

Question:

Were psychiatrists the first to recognize the value of poetry in dealing with emotional disorders?

Answer:

Yes, if you include in the term "psychiatrist" those early practitioners of the art of mental healing, known as medicine men, shamans, and witch doctors. In preliterate times and in primitive societies today reliance is placed on the power of poetry to expel illness and restore health. Through spells, incantations, invocations, and in the rites of exorcism, poetry has played and continues to perform a magical role. In tribal communities across Africa, continuing an ancient practice, the "diviner," father of mysteries, includes as a crucial element in his ritual the recitation of a special one of the 265 religio-medical poems he has been required to memorize to appeal to a particular one of 265 spirits who has victimized the patient. The medical impact of poetic language is also valued by the American Indian, by the Balinese, and in tribal communities across the globe.

Question:

It is understandable that magic spells can exert an hypnotic effect on the minds of primitive people who have been programmed to believe in them. How can poetry act comparably on present-day skeptics?

Answer:

There has been no change in man's essential nature. There has been a much greater alteration in terminology. The illness-producing forces that were externalized by our forebears as spirits, demons, etc., are now internalized as the unconscious, the subconscious, or the Id. The qualities of poetry which helped to establish communication with the supernatural are much the same as those that assist in achieving contact with our subliminal selves.

In and out of clinical practice it has become clear how often language is used for evasion. It is fascinating to observe how poetry which one tends to regard as a vehicle for fantasy is in reality the prime mode of authentic speech, welling from the deepest corners of the psyche. It is most closely in touch with our innermost condition and best reflects our essential selves. It is not beside the point that poetry has been defined as "memorable speech" (most meaningful expression), as "the best words in their best order" (most magical order) and as the psyche's true signature.

Question:

What advantage does poetry have over the other art therapies?

Answer:

All the arts are liberating, but words, the poet's amulet, constitute the lifeblood of psychotherapy and bridge more readily the distance between patient and therapist. Poetry as verbalization is also more accessible to the individual in self-therapy.

Question:

Is poetry ever countertherapeutic?

Answer:

I can think of a number of instances. When employed primarily in competition for recognition and fame, rather than self-definition, failure may trigger a serious depression. As for one given over to delusional thinking, he should not be encouraged to wander afield in the world of fantasy, which in this case could prove treacherous. A deeply disturbed individual should not be encouraged to open the Pandora's box of his unconscious without a therapist. Dante enlisted Virgil as a psychotherapist when he ventured into the Inferno.

Question:

Why are some poets hostile to the concept of poetry as a therapeutic agent?

Answer:

The term "therapy" itself has unhappy clinical connotations for many. This is unfortunate because the word is derived from the Greek word for "service" : therapeusis. Poets like Rilke believed that any psychotherapy would diminish their art. On the other hand, others like Emily Dickinson and those named above implicitly recognized therapy as a strong motivating force in their writing and discovered that it contributed considerably to the full flowering of their potential.

Question:

Have poets in the past used poetry therapeutically?

Answer:

Many, like Emily Dickinson, did so intuitively. She used poetry as therapy for herself and understood her work's therapeutic value for others. Psychiatrists today marvel how she had anticipated many of the insights of Freud into psychological dynamics and incorporated them brilliantly in her poetry. An earlier poet, Byron, in his essay *The Poet* described poetry as "the lava of the imagination whose eruption prevents the earthquake." "Poets," he wrote, "never or rarely go mad . . . but they are generally so near it, that I cannot help thinking rhyme is so far useful in anticipating and preventing the disorder."

The ranks of poets who have testified to poetry's therapeutic quality include Shakespeare, John Donne, William Blake,

Wordsworth, Robert Burns, Cardinal Newman, Robert Graves, and Schiller. Goethe wrote of his habit of converting whatever rejoiced or worried, or otherwise concerned him, into a poem, "so to have done with it, and thus at once to correct my conception of outward things and set my mind at rest."

Robert Frost has written, "Where there is doubt there is form for us to go on with. Anyone who has achieved the least form to be sure of it is lost to the larger excruciations. The artist, the poet, might be expected to be most aware of such assurances but it is really everybody's sanity to feel it and live by it."[1]

REFERENCE

1.   Frost, R. In L. Thompson, *Robert Frost: The early years.* New York: Holt, 1966, pp. 22–23.

Appendix B

INSTITUTIONS OFFERING PROGRAMS IN THE ART THERAPIES

Following are the institutions of higher education that offer 4 and more year degree programs in *art therapy, dance therapy,* and *music therapy* leading to bachelor's and master's degrees, with the B and M indicating the specific degree program(s) offered:

ART THERAPY

Albert Magnus College, New Haven, CT 06511 (B)
Anna Maria College, Paxton, MA 01612 (B)
Avila College, Kansas City, MO 64145 (B)
Buffalo State University, Buffalo, NY 14222 (M)
California State University, Sacramento, CA 95819 (M)
Capital University, Columbus, OH 43209 (B)
College of New Rochelle, New Rochelle, NY 10801 (B,M)
College of St. Teresa, Winona, MN 55987 (B)
Drake University, Des Moines, IA 50311 (B)
Edgecliff College, Cincinnati, OH 45206 (B)
Edinboro State College, Edinboro, PA 16444 (B)

Emporia State University, Emporia, KS 66801 (M)

Eureka College, Eureka, IL 61530 (B)

Fort Hays Kansas State College, Hays, KS 67601 (B)

George Washington University, Washington, DC 20052 (M)

Goddard College, Plainfield, VT 05667 (M)

Hahnemann Medical College, Philadelphia, PA 19102 (M)

Hofstra University, Hempstead, NY 11550 (M)

Immaculate Heart College, Los Angeles, CA 90027 (M)

Lake Erie College, Painesville, OH 44077 (B)

Lesley College Graduate School of Education, Cambridge, MA 02138 (M)

Lindenwood College, St. Louis, MO 65108 (M)

Lone Mountain College, San Francisco, CA 94118 (M)

Marian College, Indianapolis, IN 46222 (B)

Maryville College, St. Louis, MO 63141 (B)

Massachusetts College of Art, Boston, MA 02115 (M)

Mount Mary College, Milwaukee, WI 53222 (B)

New York University, New York, NY 10003 (B,M)

Pittsburg State University, Pittsburg, KS 66762 (B)

Pratt Institute, Brooklyn, NY 11205 (M)

Ramapo College, Mahwah, NJ 07430 (B)

Springfield College, Springfield, MA 01109 (B)

St. Thomas Aquinas College, Sparkhill, NJ 10972 (B)

Temple University, Philadelphia, PA 19140 (M)

Trenton State College, Trenton, NJ 08625 (B)

University of Bridgeport, Bridgeport, CT 06602 (B)

University of Evansville, Evansville, IN 44702 (B)

University of Houston at Clear Lake City, Houston, TX 77058 (M)

University of Louisville, Louisville, KY 40208 (M)

University of Miami, Coral Gables, FL 33124 (B)

University of Texas, Arlington, TX 76010 (M)

William James College, Grand Valley State Colleges, Allendale, MI 49401 (B)

William Woods College, Fulton, MO 65251 (B)

Wright State University, Dayton, OH 45431 (M)

Xavier University of Louisiana, New Orleans, LA 70125 (B)

If you would like additional information about careers in art therapy, write to the American Art Therapy Association, Inc., Box #11604 Pittsburg, PA 15228.

DANCE THERAPY

American University, Washington, DC 20016 (B)

Antioch–New England Graduate School, Keene, NH 03431 (M)

Goucher College, Towson, MD 21215 (B,M)

Hahnemann Medical College, Philadelphia, PA 19102 (M)

Hunter College (City University of New York), New York, NY 10021 (M)

Immaculate Heart College, Los Angeles, CA 90027 (M)

Lesley College Graduate School of Education, Cambridge, MA 02138 (M)

Lone Mountain College, San Francisco, CA 94118 (M)

Marygrove College, Detroit, MI 48203 (B)

New York University, New York, NY 10003 (B,M)

Northeastern Illinois University, Chicago, IL 60625 (B,M)

University of California at Los Angeles, CA 90024 (M)

University of Wisconsin, Madison, WI 53706 (B)

For further information about careers in dance therapy, write to the American Dance Therapy Association, 2000 Century Plaza, Columbia, MD 21044.

MUSIC THERAPY

Alverno College, Milwaukee, WI 53215 (B)

Anna Marie College, Paxton, MA 01612 (B)

Arizona State University, Tempe, AZ 85281 (B)

Augsburg College, Minneapolis, MN 55404 (B)

Baptist College at Charleston, Charleston, SC 29411 (B)

California State University, Long Beach, CA 90840 (B)

Catholic University of America, Washington, DC 20064 (B)

Clarke College, Dubuque, IA 52001 (B)

College Misericordia, Dallas, PA 18612 (B)

College of Mt. St. Joseph on the Ohio, Mt. St. Joseph, OH 45051 (B)

College of St. Teresa, Winona, MN 55987 (B)

Colorado State University, Fort Collins, CO 80523 (B)

De Paul University, Chicago, IL 60614 (B)

Duquesne University, Pittsburgh, PA 15219 (B)

East Carolina University, Greenville, NC 27834 (B)

Elizabethtown College, Elizabethtown, PA 17022 (B)

Florida State University, Tallahassee, FL 32306 (B,M)

Georgia College, Milledgeville, GA 31061 (B)

Henderson State University, Arkadelphia, AR 71923 (B)

Illinois State University, Normal, IL 61761 (B)

Indiana University at Fort Wayne, Fort Wayne, IN 46805 (B)

Loyola University, New Orleans, LA 70118 (B,M)

Maryville College, St. Louis, MO 63141 (B)

Michigan State University, East Lansing, MI 48824 (B,M)

Montclair State College, Upper Montclair, NJ 07043 (B)

Ohio University, Athens, OH 45701 (B)

Phillips University, Enid, OK 73701 (B)

Queens College, Charlotte, NC 28274 (B)

Slippery Rock State College, Slippery Rock, PA 16057 (B)

Southern Methodist University, Dallas, TX 75275 (B,M)

State University College at Fredonia, Fredonia, NY 14063 (B)

State University College at New Paltz, New Paltz, NY 12561 (B)

Texas Woman's University, Denton, TX 76204 (B,M)

University of Dayton, Dayton, OH 45469 (B)

University of Evansville, Evansville, IN 47702 (B)

University of Georgia, Athens, GA 30602 (B,M)

University of Iowa, Iowa City, IA 52242 (B)

University of Kansas, Lawrence, KS 66045 (B,M)

University of Miami, Coral Gables, FL 33124 (B,M)

University of Minnesota, Minneapolis, MN 55455 (B)

University of Missouri at Kansas City, Kansas City, MO 64111 (B)

University of the Pacific, Stockton, CA 95211 (B)

University of Wisconsin at Eau Claire, Eau Claire, WI 53201 (B)

University of Wisconsin at Milwaukee, Milwaukee, WI 53201 (B)

University of Wisconsin at Oshkosh, Oshkosh, WI 54901 (B)

Wartburg College, Waverly, IA 50677 (B)

Wayne State University, Detroit, MI 48202 (B)

West Texas State University, Canyon, TX 79016 (B)

Western Michigan University, Kalamazoo, MI 49001 (B,M)

If you would like additional information about careers in music therapy, write to the National Association for Music Therapy, P.O. Box 610, Lawrence, KS 66044.

Following are the associations that have been organized to promote *poetry therapy*.

The National Association for Poetry Therapy provides an information network to all persons interested in poetry therapy at professional, paraprofessional, patient, and agency-interface levels. It establishes ethics and standards for the training of poetry therapists as professionals, encourages research, education, and publications in the field as well as provides a link between poetry therapists. Members receive *NAPT News*, information networks. To apply for membership or secure information on certification, contact Beverly Bussolati, CPT, Secretary, NAPT, 1029 Henhawk Road, Baldwin, NY 11510.

The National Federation for Biblio/Poetry Therapy was established for educational, health, literary, and professional purposes, an umbrella organization of separate Biblio/Poetry therapy organizations. Its immediate goals are to examine qualifications for certification as poetry/bibliotherapists and to establish clear standards. President: Arleen Hynes, OSB, CPT., Box 156, St. Benedict's, St. Joseph, MN 56374.

ASCLA Bibliotherapy Forum, an organization of the American Library Association, is open to all interested in bibliotherapy. Fees include a subscription to the Newsletter and periodic membership directories. Dues are $5.00 for A.L.A. members, $7.00 for non-A.L.A. members. Make check payable to Doris Robinson, Treasurer, 6337 Manchester Drive, Parma, OH 44129.

The Association for Applied Poetry is an organization of poets, publishers, poetry therapists, and poets in the schools who apply poetry in educational, self-development and treatment programs. Founder: Jennifer Welch, 2384 Hardesty Drive South, Columbus, OH 43204.

The Bibliotherapy Round Table, a not-for-profit, nonmembership organization, provides courses, workshops, research, supervisory evaluations, and professional biblio-poetry therapy services. Contact Arleen Hynes, OSB, CPT., Box 156, St. Benedicts, St. Joseph, MN 56374.

The following provide workshops, courses, and training in *poetry therapy:*

California

At California State University, Long Beach, "Poetry and the Self" is offered at least one semester each academic year (usually in the Fall, Mondays, 7:00 to 10:00 p.m.) in the Department of English. Emphasis is on the use of poetry as catalyst and tool for personal self-awareness and as a teaching tool for students. Contact Donald J. Weinstock, Ph.D. CPT, at the University, Department of English, 1250 Bellflower Boulevard, Long Beach, CA 90840.

Poetry Therapy Institute offers workshops, courses, seminars, and lectures primarily for those in California. Director:

Arthur Lerner, Ph.D. CPT, P.O. Box 70244, Los Angeles, CA 90070.

At the University of California, Los Angeles (UCLA) Extension, Arthur Lerner, Ph.D. CPT, offers courses from time to time in "The Shape of Thought: The Psyche Through Poetry," and "Poetry and Gerontology." Contact UCLA Extension, 10995 Le Conte Avenue, Los Angeles, CA 90024, Attention: Dr. Kathryn Welds.

District of Columbia

At the Catholic University of America, Washington, DC 20064, the Department of Library and Information Science, as well as the Graduate School of Social Work, offers tutorial credits for 1 year of the part-time Bibliotherapy Training Program offered by St. Elizabeth's Hospital.

St. Elizabeth's Hospital, 2700 Martin Luther King Avenue, Washington, DC 20032 offers a 2-year, nonstipended, 440 hour program with peer groups, didactic work, and clinical experience, supported by individual and group supervision. Contact Clara Lack, M.A. CPT, or Rosalie Brown, CPT.

Florida

At Broward Community College, Pompano Beach, Ann White, CPT, offers, "Poetry and the Creative Arts as Therapy" and "The Expressive Arts as Therapy" as well as Poetry and Drama Therapy Workshops for continuing Nursing Education, Displaced Homemakers, Women in Transition, Nursing Home Activities Directors and In-Service Teacher Education Programs. Contact her at 6000 N.E. 22nd Way, Ft. Lauderdale, FL 33308.

The Department of Library Studies, University of South Florida, offers a postgraduate program in Library Studies which has a bibliotherapy component. Introductory and advanced bibliotherapy are offered, plus individual study and practicum focusing on developmental bibliotherapy. Contact Dr. Alice Smith, Department of Library Studies HMS 301, University of South Florida, Tampa, FL 33620.

Illinois

At Northwestern University, Leland H. Roloff, Ph.D., offers "Literature in the Therapeutic Setting," a survey of the historical developments in literary therapies, and of contemporary theories and the exponents, together with an examination of ways in which the theories are applied to the reading, performance, and creating of literature. Contact the Northwestern University School of Speech, The Department of Performance Studies at 1979 Sheridan Road, Evanston, IL 60201.

Kentucky

Louisville Poetry Therapy Institute offers consultations and independent studies, supervision for University of Louisville graduate students in Expressive Therapies. Contact Glenn Roosevelt, Ph.D., Co-Director, 608 Upland Road, Louisville, KY 40206.

Minnesota

At St. Cloud State University, St. Cloud, a classroom lecture-demonstration on biblio/poetry therapy is offered each semester in Reading Specialists courses by Arleen Hynes, OSB, CPT. Ms. Hynes also provides ongoing supervision and growth group experience for those who have taken a basic 50-hour introductory workshop for staff working in women's shelters in St. Cloud and St. Paul. Contact Arleen Hynes, OSB, CPT, Box 156, St. Benedicts, St. Joseph, MN 56374.

New York

Patti Feuereisen, MA, CMT, CPT, offers 2-day intensive training seminars in Poetry Therapy and the Creative Arts from time to time in Manhattan. The seminars, both informational and experiential, use a two-way mirror and video-taping. Contact Ms. Feuereisen at 237 Waverly Avenue, Brooklyn, NY 11205.

Evelyn Neinken, CPT, offers training at Gustavus Adolphus Lutheran Church, 155 East 22nd Street, Room 221, New York, NY 10010.

Hofstra University School of Education, Department of Counseling, Psychology, and Research in Education at Hempstead, NY, holds an intensive graduate course (2 credits), CPRE 283P, "Poetry Therapy for the Helping Professional" on three Sundays during the summer for the convenience of out-of-towners. Instructor is Sherry Reiter, MA, CPT, with special guests.

The New School for Social Research, 66 West 12th Street, New York, NY 10011, offers intensive seminars in "Poetry Therapy" about once a year when there is adequate registration. It is conducted by Sherry Reiter, MA, CPT, and Jack Leedy, M.D.

Ohio

The Ohio Poetry Therapy Center and Library offers individually paced programs in Audit or Certification Track with peer group and workshops, lectures and internships. Recommended training period is 2 years. A 2-week intensive Summer Colloquium of 100 hours of Poetry Therapy workshops, peer groups, panels, discussion, lectures, and research, is also offered biannually. Contact Jennifer Welch, Director, 2384 Hardesty Drive South, Columbus, OH 43204.

Kent State University (School of Library Science, Kent, OH 44242) offers a 1-week, 42-hour course for 2 graduate credits every other summer . The class is an intensive, introductory workshop taught by Rhea Rubin. For information, contact the school.

Texas

The American Academy of Poetry Therapy provides training, research and information. Director: Morris Morrison, Ph.D. 225 Congress Avenue, Suite 424, Austin, TX 78701.

At St. Edwards University, Austin, Texas, Morris Morrison, Ph.D. CPT, conducts two courses in Psychology and "Gerontology in Poetry Therapy."

At the School of Library Science, Sam Houston State University, Huntsville, a 3-hour graduate course, "Seminar in Bibliotherapy" is offered in alternating years (Spring 1986). Contact the instructor, Lesta Burt, Ph.D., at the School, P. O. Box 2236, Huntsville, TX 77341.

The National Coalition of Arts Therapies Association, 655 Fifteenth Street, N.W., Suite 300, Washington, DC 20005, was founded in 1979 and represents over 10,000 individual members and over 100 colleges and universities. It is a federation of professional organizations dedicated to the advancement of the arts as therapeutic modalities. The associations belonging to NCATA include the American Art Therapy Association, the American Association for Music Therapy, the American Dance Therapy Association, the American Society of Group Psychotherapy and Psychodrama, the National Association for Drama Therapy, and the National Association for Music Therapy.

The Coalition seeks to strengthen educational and professional bonds among arts therapies, and to foster a greater understanding of each discipline among the human service professionals and the general public. Programs sponsored by the Coalition are designed to explore how arts therapists work together, and what the future will bring in clinical practice, in research, in theory, in training, and in the political area. Another major concern is the examination of the unique contribution of the creative arts therapies, as well as their efficacy and cost-effectiveness.

INDEX